The Simplified Stagecraft Manual

The Simplified Stagecraft Manual

by
LEROY STAHL

Publishers
T. S. DENISON & COMPANY, INC.
Minneapolis

CONTENTS

Chapter I

SCENE BUILDING

There is no satisfactory substitute for well built and well painted stage scenery. This volume aims to choose the best professional methods and adapt them to the needs of the amateur who wishes to do a workmanlike job in all the technical departments of the theatre.

Although the limitations of a modest budget have been kept in mind, one thing should be remembered. There is no real economy in flimsy, poorly constructed stage scenery. It should be built to regular stage standards. Proper construction guarantees that stage scenery will give the maximum amount of service over the longest period of time, provided it receives adequate care.

Prices on the materials suggested have not been quoted because these vary from time to time in different localities. All materials have been selected from the viewpoint of good service over a long period of time. Should any item reach beyond the purse of the amateur producer, the expense should be budgeted over several productions. There is no other way of making permanent, lasting, and economical additions to stage equipment.

If this volume can save some organization five hundred dollars by showing that there is no real necessity for purchasing an elaborately painted, antiquated, and expensive woodland drop and set of woodwings, one of its major purposes will have been accomplished. Together, all the stage equipment described in the following pages, can be built for much less than the cost of such an outmoded "white elephant."

The Stage

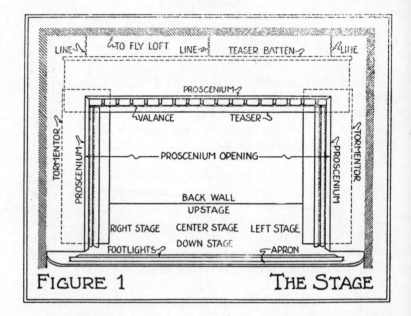

FIGURE 1   THE STAGE

Although dimensions vary, there are certain descriptive terms applicable to any stage. The embryo scene technician should learn the professional language. A study of the accompanying diagram (Fig. 1) should be made by any person not already familiar with stage terminology and its meaning. It will be noted that such directions as *right stage* and *left stage* are always given from the viewpoint of the actor or the person who faces the audience. *Downstage* is toward the audience, *upstage* away from it. The space above the stage is known as the *fly loft*. The "picture frame" through which the audience views the play is known as the *proscenium opening*. Its boundaries form the *proscenium* or the *proscenium arch*. If any additional terms are not understood, the text will clarify their meaning.

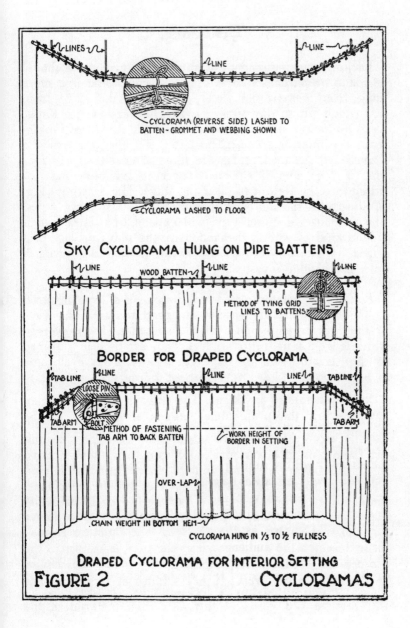

CYCLORAMA (REVERSE SIDE) LASHED TO
BATTEN - GROMMET AND WEBBING SHOWN

CYCLORAMA LASHED TO FLOOR

SKY CYCLORAMA HUNG ON PIPE BATTENS

LINE   WOOD BATTEN   LINE   LINE

METHOD OF TYING GRID
LINES TO BATTENS

BORDER FOR DRAPED CYCLORAMA

TAB LINE   LINE   LINE   LINE   TAB LINE

LOOSE PIN

TAB ARM   BOLT   METHOD OF FASTENING
TAB ARM TO BACK BATTEN   WORK HEIGHT OF
BORDER IN SETTING   TAB ARM

OVER-LAP

CHAIN WEIGHT IN BOTTOM HEM
CYCLORAMA HUNG IN ⅓ TO ½ FULLNESS

DRAPED CYCLORAMA FOR INTERIOR SETTING

FIGURE 2   CYCLORAMAS

Cycloramas

Lacking stage equipment of any kind, a cyclorama should be made or purchased first of all. A cyclorama is a cloth hung from *battens* completely encircling the stage from downstage left to downstage right. They are of two kinds, a *sky cyclorama* used in exterior scenes, and a *draped cyclorama* for interior scenes. The latter is sometimes called a *draped set.* All cycloramas are hung from either *wood* or *pipe battens,* and if sufficient space is available, may be raised into the fly loft to clear the stage. The drawing (Fig. 2) illustrates the major differences between the two types. The purchase of either type will depend to a large extent on the kind of setting demanded by the plays usually produced. If exterior settings are never used, a sky "cyc" is naturally a poor investment.

Borders, or narrow pieces of cloth of the same material as the cyclorama, are spaced overhead to *mask* any view of the *flies* from the eyes of the audience. Their average width is from four feet to six feet. They are used in a draped set, and usually, two are required. Ideally, a sky cyclorama is high enough to be used without borders.

Sky cycloramas: Cycloramas may be bought, sometimes quite cheaply, but they may be made at home just as well. Usually, sky cycloramas are made either of light blue outing flannel or of heavy muslin or canvas. Flannel is satisfactory but tears easily. It should not be used without a backing of some other material such as Indian Head muslin. If the cyclorama is made of canvas (10 or 12 oz. white duck) or heavy muslin, it should be painted a light turquoise or cerulian blue.

Most amateur stages have openings ranging from 25 to 30 feet. For a stage of this width, a convenient size for the cyclorma would be 24 feet high by 48 feet long. It will require 128 yards of thirty-six inch material in the construction. Sky cycloramas are sewed with a *lapped seam*, that is, the two selvedged edges of the cloth are laid flat on top of each other and then sewed twice, once down the outer edge of each selvedge. At least a three-eighths inch over-lapping of the cloth is necessary for strength. Cycloramas of this type always hang better if the seams run parallel to the floor instead of up and down. A good, heavy linen thread should be used in sewing any material for the stage. A six-inch hem should be sewed on both the top and bottom of the cyclorama and a one-inch hem on each end.

Draped Cycloramas: Draped cycloramas are made of either *duvetyne, repp* or *velour*. *Sateen* may be used on occasion but it tears easily and is not satisfactory without lining for any permanent stage installation. *Monk's cloth* has been a great favorite for stage hangings, but due to its somewhat higher price, its popularity is fading in favor of repp and duvetyne. Velour is expensive but it does possess a richness not found in the other materials. Repp and duvetyne are very serviceable, look well under stage lighting, and are reasonable in price. Duvetyne is the cheaper of the two, but it is harder to keep clean and is more easily torn. Duvetyne is available in a wide range of colors with silver gray being the most adaptable for general stage use. Two colors of repp are used usually in stage cycloramas, natural and light gray. The latter is preferable because long usage imparts a faintly mouldy color to the natural shade. A draped cyclorama setting of light gray in either repp or duvetyne is the most serviceable acquisition that can be made by the average amateur group. A play can be adequately mounted in such a setting with little more than the necessary furniture and properties.

Draped cycloramas are made with either *one-third* or *one-half fullness*. In one-third fullness, four inches out of every foot of material across the top of the drape are used in making the folds. In one-half fullness, six inches are used. The method of making these folds is illustrated in Fig. 3a.

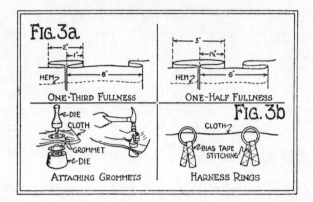

It is necessary to take into account the extra material required for these folds when ordering cloth for a draped cyclorama. Also, if the cyclorama is made in sections, it will be necessary to add to the bill enough material to allow these sections to *over-lap* at least six inches. Allowance must also be made for a hem of good size on both the top and the bottom.

The following material order is given for a draped cyclorama fourteen feet high, with the *back wall* eighteen feet long, and with each *side wall* twelve feet long. The back wall is made in two ten-foot sections to allow for an over-lap at each end and in the center. Including the hems, it will take five yards of material to make the cyclorama fourteen feet high. Therefore, each side wall requires twenty yards of thirty-six inch material plus another forty-eight inch by five yards piece on each side wall to allow for the extra fullness. In like manner, each section of the back wall will require a piece five yards high by fourteen inches wide to allow for the one-third fullness. Two *interior borders* will require eighteen yards of forty-eight inch material if they are simply hemmed along one selvedged edge and hung lengthwise across the stage. Thus, the entire bill for material will include some ninety yards of either thirty-six inch repp or duvetyne plus twenty-eight yards of forty-eight inch repp or duvetyne.

Sew the cloth together by using pieces five yards long until each section is the required width. Then sew a six-inch hem across the top and bottom of each section. While sewing, be sure that all seams and hems are on the reverse side of the cyclorama. This last may seem a pointless suggestion, but the person who can sew a large cyclorama without at least one mistake possesses genius.

Rigging: All cycloramas are hung on battens. The simplest method is to tack them in place, but this practice should be discouraged as it eventually tears the cloth. In the best method, a strip of *jute webbing* three and a half inches wide is sewed across the top and *grommets* inserted, but one-inch harness rings are just as satisfactory. These are sewed firmly into place by using short pieces of *bias tape*. These may be doubled for extra strength. Both methods are shown in Fig. 3b. *Tie lines* of one-eighth inch cotton cord are tied into either the grommets or rings and *lashed* to the batten as shown in the little drawing inserted at the top of Fig. 2. It is best to equip a sky cyclorama with the same arrangement of either grommets or rings on its bottom edge so that this too may be lashed to a batten (Fig. 2). With the bottom batten lashed securely to the floor, the whole cyclorama can be kept smooth and free from wrinkles. An ordinary iron or steel chain or a series of heavy washers are sewed in the bottom hem of a draped cyclorama to give it the weight to hang nicely.

Many stage technicians are guilty of an objectionable practice in connection with draped cycloramas. When an opening is required for a door or window, they rip open a seam. It is much better to provide for such eventualities when the cyclorama is made by closing certain seams with ordinary dress hooks and eyes or snaps instead of sewing them. This method is neater and adds to the life of the cyclorama.

Fireproofing: Cycloramas can be flameproofed by spraying them or dipping them in a solution composed of one pound of borax and one pound of sal ammoniac dissolved in one gallon of water. They should be hung on the battens to dry and ironed afterwards if it is necessary. Needless to say, if a sky cyclorama is to be painted, the flame-proofing process must be taken care of before any paint is applied to the canvas. This fireproofing mixture may be used on any type of scenery as may also one pound of powdered alum dissolved in a gallon of water. Scene pigment itself is fireproof and may be used on flat scenery in place of either one of the above solutions.

Battens

Wooden Battens: When a batten is divided into three sections as it is in the bottom drawing of Fig. 2, the two short battens on each end of the *back batten* are known as *side* or *tab arms*. Lines from the loft attached to the ends of the tab arms are called *tab lines*. When the cyclorama is *flied* or raised to clear the stage, the tab arms usually hang free while the excess drapery hanging below the bottom edge of the back wall is bundled loosely into a huge knot. Battens should be attached to the *fly lines* so the width of the batten hangs perpendicular to the floor. This prevents splitting or breaking of the batten.

Battens are made of one inch by four inch white pine. The pieces of stock are *staggered* in construction. A twenty-foot batten is made of four ten-foot pieces. One side will be composed of two ten-foot pieces joined end to end while the other side will have one ten-foot piece in the center covering the previous joint and a five-foot piece on each end. The lumber is fastened together by using one and one-quarter inch No. 9 wood screws. A more workmanlike job can be accomplished by rounding off the edges of the batten with a carpenter's plane.

Pipe Battens: Pipe battens are made of one and one-quarter inch or one and one-half inch iron pipe. The sections are fastened together with *pipe couplings*. In the case of sky cycloramas, pipe battens are usually bent at the corners in an arc to allow the cyclorama to hang without wrinkles at these places. If pipe battens are used an a drape cyclorama, flexible *fittings* are available at theatrical supply houses for allowing the tab arms to swing freely in any direction. These are really necessary to make a suitable joint at the corners.

Doors—Windows—Fireplaces

Doors and windows may be indicated in a cyclorama setting by drawing openings in the cloth, but the more ambitious stage craftsman will want to build these architectural features. All doors, windows, and fireplaces should be built of such size that they may be later incorporated into a *box setting* constructed of *flats* and *wings*. The planning of every piece of scenery as a unit of a larger setting should begin the moment a piece of lumber is sawed. A huge, clumsy set of doors too large to fit in any box setting will only gather dust in the store room after their initial appearance. All *units* of constructed scenery should be made *to work* interchangeably with other units already built or with those that may be built in the future.

Doors: Stage doors used to be made of canvas stretched over a wooden frame. A much more satisfactory and substantial door is shown in Fig. 4a. In brief, this door is made of a wooden frame backed by a piece of *Champion Board*. The frame-work is constructed as in any door with the exception that both the frame and the door itself need be finished only on one side if it is planned to have the door open *offstage*. Sometimes, light, well-constructed house doors can be bought from lumber dealers or mill work supply houses. If a real bargain is available, it may be cheaper to buy a door than to build one, but in either case, it will be necessary to build the frame.

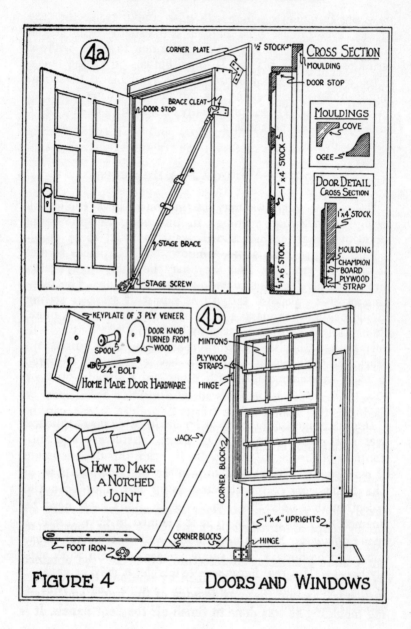

FIGURE 4   DOORS AND WINDOWS

The standard dimensions of an interior door are two feet six inches by six feet six inches, but for stage purposes, a door three feet wide will prove more practical. The door illustrated is known as the *six panel type*. The framework, with the exception of the bottom *rail*, is constructed of one inch by four inch white pine. The bottom rail is made of a piece of one inch by six inch white pine. Stock ordered in these dimensions will be a trifle skimpy so allowance must be made for the fractional differences in the width of the lumber when it is sawed. The pieces are fastened together on the back of the board by using three-fourths inch by five-eighths inch *corrugated fasteners*. Three or four will be sufficient for each joint. A piece of Champion Board large enough to cover the entire frame is then tacked across the back. Should more strength be needed, the door can be reinforced by nailing *straps* of one-fourth inch *plywood* across the back of the joints. The inside edge of the panels can be made more attractive by either beveling them off with a plane or by fitting in either *cove* or *ogee mouldings* as shown in the drawing.

Door *hardware*, such as hinges and handles, should be purchased from a hardware store, but wooden door handles can be made on occasion. The *key plate* can be cut from a piece of one-fourth inch plywood, a wooden spool may be used for the shank, while a small wooden circle can be rounded off to serve as a knob. The whole is fitted together with a long bolt and painted a suitable color. (Fig. 4b).

The outside frame (the casing) of the door, is built of one inch by six inch white pine stock. The construction is clearly shown in Fig. 4a. Door *stops* may be provided by nailing strips of *lattice stock* on the inside of the door frame. The face of the door frame or the trim may be left plain, but a more interesting architectural effect may be obtained by nailing strips of one-half inch by one and three-quarter inch stock around the outside edge of the frame and inserting moulding as was done to finish off the door panels. It is advisable to use at least two-inch screws in building this type of door frame. Nails will pull out at critical times if used in the main framework. If necessary for strength, cover the joints with flat steel *corner plates* on the reverse side of the construction. These may be bought at any hardware store. The three-inch or four-inch size is large enough.

Jacks and Braces: When used in a draped setting, a door such as the above is held in position by using *stage braces*, one on each side of the frame. This very valuable piece of equipment is shown in the drawing, although *jacks* (a jack is shown with the window) can be made at home, cost less than stage braces, and are just as efficient. Jacks are fastened to scenery by means of *loose pin hinges*. One-half of the hinge is fastened to the scenery, the other half to the jack. They are held together by dropping a nail through the two halves. A one and one-half inch *back flap hinge* can be made into a loose pin hinge by cutting out the *tight pin* with a hack saw. The *foot iron* used on a jack is simply a piece of *strap iron* with a hole bored in one end large enough for a *stage screw* to be inserted.

Windows: A window to be used with a draped setting is diagrammed in Fig. 4b. Stage windows are constructed very much in the manner of a regular house window except that they need be finished only on one side and usually require no glass. The window sashes are constructed of one inch by three inch white pine. The window *muntons* are made of stock sawed to three-quarter inch by three-quarter inch. They are fastened to the window sashes by using small plywood straps. A better window results if each munton runs the full length or width of each window section. To do this, a *notched joint* should be used where the muntons cross. It is advisable to make the front trim of the window match that of the door as closely as possible. If the window is not *practical*, that is, if it is not necessary to raise or lower the individual sashes, they may be nailed in place. If they are to be raised, each sash should be provided with a groove by nailing small pieces of lattice stock to the side of the sills.

A simple window may be made by stretching canvas over the frame and painting the muntons on it. After the paint has dried, the remaining portion of the canvas is cut away with a razor blade. This method, however, is not to be recommended except as a makeshift in an emergency.

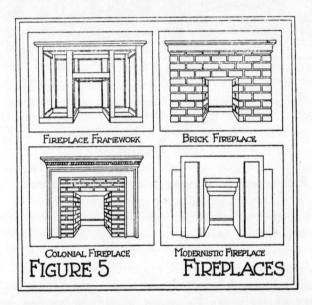

FIREPLACE FRAMEWORK   BRICK FIREPLACE

COLONIAL FIREPLACE   MODERNISTIC FIREPLACE

FIGURE 5   FIREPLACES

Fireplaces: Fireplaces are made by constructing a light wooden frame of one inch by two inch white pine in the shape desired and then covering it with either muslin or Champion Board. Architectural decorations, such as mouldings, are added afterwards by tacking them on with light *brads* or *finishing nails*. A framework together with several very usable styles of fireplaces is to be seen in Fig. 5. When used with a cyclorama, fireplaces are held in an upright position by using a stage brace or a jack. In a box setting, they may be fastened to the scenery with screen door *hooks and eyes* or with loose pin hinges. If a brick fireplace is desired, an excellent method of making artistic looking bricks is detailed in the section devoted to special effects.

"GIANTS IN THE EARTH"   ACT II   "THRU THE KEYHOLE"   ACT I
FIGURE 6   CUT DOWN SCENERY

Set Pieces

A well organized scenery plan designed to answer the needs of an amateur producing group over a period of years does not always include the use of *set pieces,* but there are plays where their use cannot be avoided. A set piece is any piece of scenery which "sets" by itself on the stage. It may be a house, a distant castle, or a clump of bushes. However, by combining set pieces with *cut down* scenery, almost any number of plays can be staged providing the designer is willing that the productions restrict themselves to certain very decided limitations. Cut down scenery is used in conjunction with a cyclorama and may be used with equal effectiveness for either an interior or exterior setting. The object of such cut down or "suggestive" scenery is to show the main features of a setting and at the same time employ as little heavy construction as possible. The drawing (Fig. 6) shows the use of cut down scenery in an interior setting.

The walls of interior settings similar to the above may be called *screens*. The setting for the bedroom scene of "Giants in the Earth" is designed to be not over eight or nine feet high. The walls are *stippled* to resemble rough, painted plaster while overhead are crudely sawed beams of an early pioneer home. Such beams are, of course, lightly built and need be finished only on two sides, the front and bottom.

The setting for "Thru the Keyhole" uses three modernistic screens about ten feet high. The two screens on each side are hinged at their upstage corner while the one used behind the center openings extends across the stage parallel to the footlights. An excellent color scheme for this setting would be a rather neutral olive-green for the walls with the line decorations painted the color of burnished copper.

The construction of such screens or of set pieces will be more readily understood after reading the section devoted to flat scenery.

Flat Scenery

Flat scenery is at once the chief joy and most potent source of trouble for the amateur stage technician. Properly built and well handled, no other type of scenery gives the same feeling of solidity resulting from the use of *flats* and *wings*. They have demonstrated their supreme usefulness through several decades of theatrical history, and despite the howls of some enraged "Art" groups still remain the most practical method of staging a play.

Wings are light but sturdily built frames of wood covered with cloth and painted. Flats are several wings joined or *battened* together to form a single wall of a box setting, although in the loosely applied terminology of the theatre, individual wings are sometimes known as flats. Wings must be easily handled, must fit with other wings, take little space when stored, and have no sharp projections to mar or

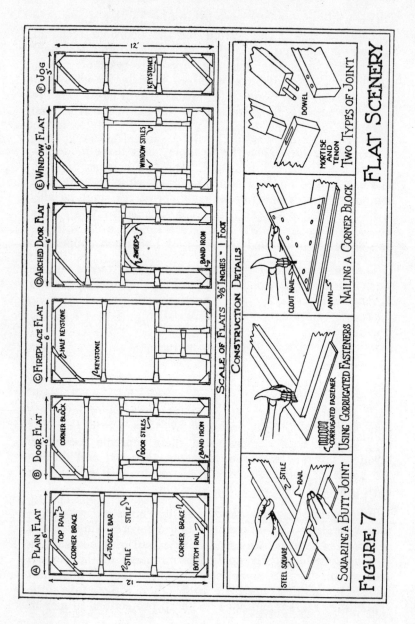

FIGURE 7

FLAT SCENERY

tear the painted surface of any other wing when they are *packed* together against a wall.

Each individual piece of a flat or wing has its own name. The long pieces of lumber which form the sides of a flat are known as *stiles*. The top and bottom pieces are referred to as the *top* and *bottom rails*. Pieces on the interior of the frame running parallel to the floor are called *toggle rails, toggle bars,* or simply *toggles*. Light pieces set at a forty-five degree angle across the corners of a flat are known as *corner braces. Door* or *window stiles* are used when a flat carries an opening for either one of these pieces. The construction of typical flat pieces is clearly shown in Fig. 7.

Most stage scenery is built of one inch by three inch Idaho white pine of No. 1 grade, although if reasonably straight and clear pieces of either the No. 2 or 3 grades are available, they may be used. If rigid economy must be practiced, it is better to make the stiles out of the best grade of lumber and cut the rails and toggle bars from the cheaper grades. Good lumber in the stiles helps keep them from warping and thus prevents the occurence of cracks or *holidays* between the finished flats.

Dimensions: Flats may be constructed of any size as convenience or necessity dictates, but it is not advisable to make any flat wider than six feet. The stage technician who builds a flat wider than six feet is apt to find himself in the position of the man who built a boat in his basement. There will be no door wide enough to carry it through. If single surfaces wider than six feet are necessary, it is wiser to make them by hinging two smaller sections together so that they may be folded for handling. Flats less than four feet wide are termed *jogs*. A height of twelve feet is a good, workable dimension on most small stages although on larger ones, a height of fourteen feet has many great advantages.

Cutting: The actual dimensions of one inch by three inch lumber are three-fourths inch thick by two and five-eighths inches wide. These measurements must be taken into account before it is cut. It is more convenient to cut the top and bottom rails first. These are made the full width of the flat. The stiles are cut to a length of twelve feet minus two widths of the lumber used in the rails. Stiles are always fitted with their butt end against the rails. Unless this is done, the stile is likely to split as the flat is dragged across the floor. Toggle bars are cut the width of the flat minus two widths of the lumber used in making the stiles. It will be noted that lumber purchased from the yards is usually finished only on three sides. One edge will be roughly sawed. This unfinished surface should be either planed smooth or placed so that it appears only on the interior of the flat construction.

Assembling: In assembling a flat, the lumber is laid on the floor in the position it occupies in the finished product as shown in Fig. 7. Before fastening any joint, the builder must make sure it is absolutely square by checking it with a carpenter's steel square held on the outside edge of the construction. This is done to avoid cracks between the flats. They are certain to appear unless each flat is absolutely square.

On twelve-foot scenery, a butt *joint* is strong enough for most purposes. A butt joint is made by first nailing the stock together with corrugated fasteners (Fig. 7). A *corner block* of one-quarter inch three-ply white pine veneer is then nailed over the joint with one and one-quarter inch *clout nails*. A sheet metal plate called an *anil* is placed underneath the work while the nailing is done. This automatically clinches the clout nail on the face of the flat and insures a tight joint. Corner blocks are made by cutting a ten-inch square of wood veneer diagonally from corner to corner. For best results, the grain on the outside of the corner block should run parallel to the grain of the stile. Toggle bars are fastened in exactly the same way except that a saving in veneer can be effected by using *keystones* in place of corner blocks. These are eight inches long and shaped as shown in Fig. 7. In nailing both keystones and corner blocks, the clout nails should be staggered to avoid splitting the wood. Also, it is advisable to place the keystones and corner blocks in about one-quarter inch from the edges of the flat to avoid snagging them on other pieces of scenery. Corner braces are fashioned from one inch by two inch white pine and are fastened in place by *half keystones*, or a regulation sized keystone ripped down the middle. Keystones should be cut with the outside grain of the wood running the long way. Keystones and corner blocks may also be fastened to the flat with strong carpenter's glue before the nailing is done, but this is not strictly necessary.

Door, window and *fireplace flats* are constructed in the same manner except that openings must be provided for these pieces. It is well to make these openings at least one-half inch longer and wider in the case of doors and windows to allow them to fit more easily. Doors or windows are held firmly in the flat by means of a six or eight inch *strap hinge* placed at a slight angle on the *thickness* of their outside frame. Fig. 9 shows the method.

In door flats, the bottom rail is cut away from the opening and a *band* iron inserted. Band irons are cut from straps of iron three-quarter inch wide by one-eighth inch thick. They extend about six inches beyond the opening of the door on each side and are drilled for one and one-half inch No. 9 screws. It may be necessary to round the ends of each band iron with a file to prevent any sharp edges from cutting the floor while the flat is dragged along.

Plugs are sometimes made so that they may be fitted into the door or window openings thus allowing these pieces to be used as plain flats. These are built like a small flat and must fit very snugly. They are held in place by *window buttons* screwed on the back of the flats (Fig. 9).

Hardware: It is much easier to fasten the necessary hardware on a flat before the canvas is *stretched* over the frame.

Lash lines are placed in the inside upper right hand corner of every flat. Cotton *sash cord* of the one-fourth inch size makes the best lash line. A *lash cleat* is fastened on the left hand side of the flat about a foot below the *lash line eye* on the other side. Additional lash cleats are placed on the flat as shown in Fig. 9. All such hardware is available in a specialized form at theatrical supply houses, but substitutions can be made from the regular stock carried by most hardware stores. Small *screw eyes* can be made to serve as lash line eyes. It is possible to use one and one-half or two inch *round headed screws* in place of lash cleats. However, such screws should not be inserted without drilling first as they may split the lumber. A No. 2 screw eye will serve very well in place of the *brace cleat* illustrated in the drawing. Most hardware stores carry a kind of screen window *hanger* which can be made into an excellent substitute for either brace or lash cleats. They are very reasonable in price. They fasten in place with small screws and have several advantages over the use of large screw eyes or screws.

Stretching: The cloth covering on scenery is known as the *stretch*. A better grade of Indian Head or unbleached muslin is excellent for most purposes. Muslin can be obtained in widths sufficient to cover almost any size flat. If it must be sewed, the seams should be made to run the length of the flat *i. e.* up and down.

Scenery is *stretched* by laying the muslin over the flat and first tacking it lightly in place on the inside of each corner. The stretching begins at the center of each stile and works toward the corners. The tacks are driven about six or eight inches apart and about one-fourth inch in from the inside edge of the frame. Afterwards, the ends of the flat are stretched in the same manner, that is, from the center of the rails to the outside corner. The muslin is kept smooth but should not be pulled too tightly. A little *bounce* should always be left in the cloth. When all sides of the flat have been stretched, the tacks are pulled out of the corners and any wrinkles removed before tacking the corners for the last time. No. 4 *carpet tacks* are the best to use on scenery.

The remainder of the cloth is glued to the frame by using a mixture of water, *whiting,* and melted *gelatine glue* mixed to the consistency of heavy cream. To each gallon of water and whiting mixed to the proper consistency, two and one-half cups of the melted glue are added. There are prepared pastes which may be used for this type of gluing, but on scenery, a little additional melted glue should be added for the sake of safety. When the glue is dry, the excess cloth is trimmed back with a razor blade to about one-eighth inch from the outside edge of the flat.

Backings

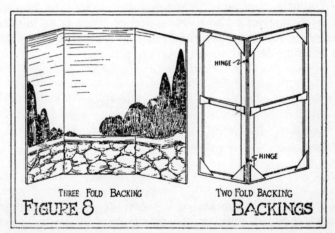

THREE FOLD BACKING

TWO FOLD BACKING

FIGURE 8   BACKINGS

Backings (Fig. 8) may be made in either two or three sections. In reality, they are short flats hinged together down one side. The hinges (two-inch *back flaps*) are screwed on the face of the flat. The purpose of the hinging is to allow the two painted surfaces of the flats to come together when the backing is *booked* or folded and to allow the backing to stand by itself without bracing when used behind an opening in the set. The hinges are inset into the lumber so that they do not project from the surface of the flat. Two or three are required for each backing. A narrow strip of cloth is glued over the joint to cover the hinges and any crack which might otherwise appear between the sections of the backing.

Backings may be made with a painted surface on both sides of the individual flats by using *two way hinges* at the joints. When this is done, keystones and corner blocks cannot be used in the construction. By using either *mortised and tenoned* or *doweled* joints, muslin can be stretched smoothly over the reverse side and painted equally well. (Fig. 7).

Backings are used behind all openings in the setting and are, therefore, called either *door backings, window backings,* or *fireplace backings*. They may be painted to represent either an interior or an exterior scene. There is no standard height for backings, but they must be high enough to mask the opening behind which they are placed.

Assembling a Setting

After a set of flat scenery has been built, the next problem is to put it together. This should not be especially difficult if care has been exercised in the planning and building.

Lashing: Flats are *lashed* together as detailed in Fig. 9. The method of making the *tie-off knot* is shown in the little inserted drawing. Such a knot pulls the lash line as tight as possible and has the added virtue of coming untied merely by giving the end of the line a slight jerk. It is advisable to dip the end of each lash line in glue to prevent fraying. The busy little gentleman who goes around tying knots in the end of lash lines for this purpose has no place on any stage. Such knots invariably snarl the lash lines and complicate the process of shifting scenery

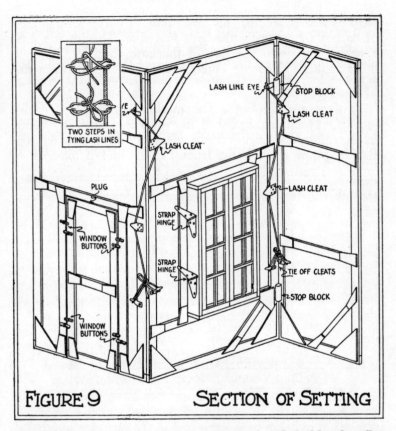

FIGURE 9   SECTION OF SETTING

decidedly. An expert *grip* or stage hand holds the flat to be lashed with his left hand on the toggle bar. With his right hand, he *snaps* the lash line over the top cleat of the next flat and then completes the lashing by pulling the line as tight as possible and finishing off with the knot.

Old flats, or those that are badly warped, should be planed until they fit together without cracks at the joints. Badly warped flats may be hinged together and a strip of cloth glued over the joint as recommended for backings. On most amateur stages, this latter method is advisable for even new scenery unless it possesses a *lip*. Such scenery has a strip of veneer, a "lip," set in a *rabbeted* cut down one side of each flat, generally the lash line side. The lip fits into a rabbet cut down the side of the adjoining flat. Both of these methods eliminate objectionable holidays between the flats.

Borders and Ceilings: The masking of the top of the setting may be accomplished in two ways, either by using *interior borders* or a *ceiling piece*. Interior borders are flat strips of cloth hung from battens and painted in a

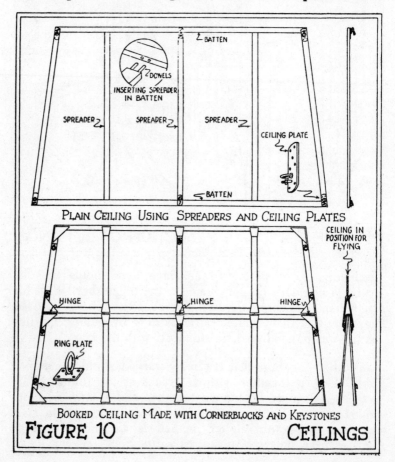

PLAIN CEILING USING SPREADERS AND CEILING PLATES

BOOKED CEILING MADE WITH CORNERBLOCKS AND KEYSTONES

FIGURE 10   CEILINGS

neutral shade that matches the setting, but ceilings are recommended in every case where they can be used.

The operation of a ceiling is not as difficult as it might at first appear. A ceiling makes the stage setting much more substantial and has the further advantage of acting as a sounding board for the voices of the actors.

Ceilings are of two types, *booked* and *plain*. A plain ceiling is built very much like a large flat but large enough to cover the entire top of the setting. Booked ceilings are built in two sections and fold or *book* across their centers in a line running parallel to the footlights. Fig. 10 illustrates the major differences between the two types and their construction.

Occasionally, the *spreaders,* or what would be the toggle bars of a ceiling, are made removable so that the whole may be rolled and stored away. In these cases, the spreaders are bolted in place by means of *ceiling plates* obtainable from theatrical hardware dealers. *Ring bolts* are used for attaching the lines when this is not done. It is possible to insert spreaders into the frame of a ceiling by using loose doweled joints as illustrated in Fig. 10.

Ceilings are hung in place before the set is put up, and then, lightly dropped to the top of the flats and tied off. If scenery is changed during the performance, it is necessary to raise the ceiling only a foot or so to clear the tops of the flats. After the ceiling is lowered, minor discrepancies in the fit of the flats can sometimes be corrected by pushing them together and allowing the weight of the ceiling to hold them in place.

The Exterior Setting

Beyond doubt, more horrible montrosities have been inflicted upon the theatre going public under the guise of an exterior setting than anything seen upon the stage. The day, however, is happily gone when a painted back drop in the best style of the Mid-Victorian theatre and a set of violent and unnatural wood wings constitute an acceptable exterior setting.

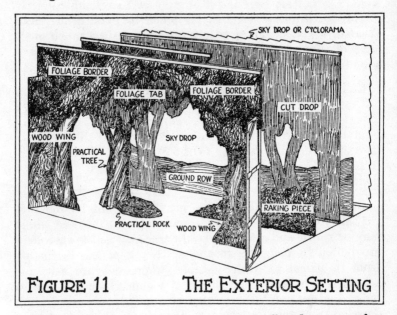

FIGURE 11 — THE EXTERIOR SETTING

The above drawing is by no means offered as a perfect exterior setting. It is merely a plan to show the various elements customarily used in stage exteriors. It should be remembered that a few well-designed and well-executed scenic pieces make a better exterior setting than a stage swarming with every imaginable kind of foliage, rocks or trees.

The basis of all exterior settings is the *sky drop* or the sky cyclorama. The sky drop is similar to the cyclorama except that it has no tab arms. It simply runs straight across the stage in back of the setting. In practice, it usually is not as long nor as high as a sky cyclorama.

Borders and Tabs: Foliage borders and *foliage tabs* are flat pieces of cloth hung from battens. A foliage border covers the entire width of the stage while a foliage tab is used in special instances and covers only a fraction of the width of the stage. Very rarely are they less than six feet wide. The bottom edge is cut or *profiled* to resemble masses of foliage. Borders and tabs are made by tacking the cloth between the two halves of a batten before it has been assembled. The cutting of the profiled edge is not done until after the painting.

Ground Rows: A *raking piece* is really a short *ground row.* It does not cover the whole width of the stage and acquires its name from the fact that it is placed on the stage at a *rake* or slight angle. A ground row most often forms the horizon line of an exterior setting while a raking piece serves to indicate small masses of foliage or topographical features in the foreground.

Both are constructed in the manner of extremely short flats. The top edge is profiled by tacking one-fourth inch veneer or *Cornell Board** and cutting it to the shape desired. A neater job will result if the frame of the flat construction is rabbeted back about one and one-half inches from the outside edge to a depth of one-quarter inch. This is done on the face of the flat. The veneer or composition board is nailed into place with *barrel nails* or short *roofing nails.* Careful scene builders cut *profiling* with the outside edge at a slight bevel on the reverse side. Cutting in this fashion gives what is known as a "feather edge" and prevents the audience from seeing the thickness of the material.

Cut Drops: Excellent effects can be achieved in an exterior through the use of a *cut drop.* The one shown in the drawing (Fig. 11) is composed of two *legs* and, strictly

---

*The terms "Cornell Board" and "Champion Board" used in this volume are trade names used to designate a composition board of a certain type. Identical material may be available under another name (Upson Board). There are many varieties of composition board. A great many of them are not suitable for the uses described.

speaking, is a leg drop. A true cut drop would cover the full width of the stage. Either type can be used as the occasion demands. Quite frequently, cut drops are used only to show the silhouettes of trees. They are not elaborately painted. The cut out portions of the drop are removed after the painting is done. A more substantial cut drop can be made by backing these openings with *netting* or *theatrical gauze*. Heavy gauze is sometimes available at local drapery stores, but usually, it must be ordered from theatrical dealers. It is fastened to the back of the drop with a special glue (Rosine) prepared for the purpose or by the mixture used in gluing canvas to the flat frames mentioned previously. Rosine is a flexible glue and will not crack if the drop is rolled for storing.

Woodwings: The harsh, stiff looking woodwings of the old school are chiefly responsible for the disapproval usually reserved for this item of stage scenery. Such woodwings are not designed from the standpoint of good sense. They are generally drawn with the tree trunks averaging no more than three or four feet in height. The scenic artist must then make his woodwing as wide as the overtowering mass of a tree's foliage or chop it off prematurely. The latter is the usual course with the result that some very fantastic appearing trees are seen on the stage. If, on the other hand, the tree trunks are drawn somewhere near their natural height of eight or ten feet this difficulty is obviated. The spreading foliage is taken care of by the foliage border. The tree trunk alone, perhaps a few of the lower branches, forms the profiled edge of the woodwing. Naturally, the foliage border should not be chopped off squarely either. The foliage masses should descend from a high point near the center of the stage and drop naturally and gracefully to the top of the woodwings and binding the stage picture in natural, correctly handled foliage. A little study of Fig. 11 will make this point clear.

Woodwings are hinged together in the same manner as backings. The profiled edge of Cornell Board or veneer runs up and down the inside edge of the onstage wing. It is fastened into place and cut in the way previously described for ground rows and raking pieces.

The construction of woodwings and other exterior pieces is relatively simple once the general method of scene building has been mastered. The painting is the difficult thing. A method of painting acceptable foliage is outlined in the section devoted to scene painting.

Practical Rocks and Trees

The construction of all rounded or irregular shaped objects on the stage follows one general formula. First, a wooden frame is built roughly to the shape finally desired. Over this is tacked a little weight, fairly fine meshed *chicken wire*. This is hammered to the shape desired in the finished product. Strips of cloth or heavy *building paper* are then dipped in glue, applied to the netting, and allowed to harden. The rock or tree is then painted in the color desired.

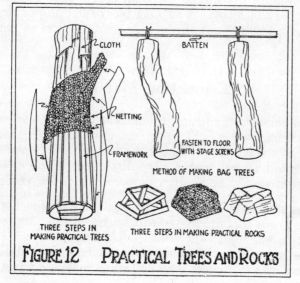

CLOTH   BATTEN

NETTING

FRAMEWORK

FASTEN TO FLOOR WITH STAGE SCREWS

METHOD OF MAKING BAG TREES

THREE STEPS IN MAKING PRACTICAL TREES

THREE STEPS IN MAKING PRACTICAL ROCKS

FIGURE 12   PRACTICAL TREES AND ROCKS

Both rocks and trees together with the main points to be observed in their construction is illustrated in Fig. 12. In building a tree, three wooden circles are cut of the size desired and strips of one inch by three inch white pine are nailed to them. If any limbs or gnarled spots are desired on the tree, these are cut from wider pieces of lumber and nailed or screwed in the proper place. Stage trees are left open at the back to allow them to be braced with a jack .or a stage brace. In applying the glue on saturated paper or cloth for the bark, it must be remembered to wrinkle it in as close an approximation to the bark of an actual tree as possible.

It is not always necessary to make rocks or trees as substantial as the foregoing. There is a type of stage tree known as the *bag tree*. This is a long bag of cloth with a wooden circle at each end to give it shape. They are made by taking a piece of cloth of the required size, painting it wildly with any number of colors, and twisting the whole thing into a long, sausage-like knot. When the paint is dry, the cloth is pried apart and tacked to the wooden circles. The resulting wrinkles in the cloth bear a close resemblance to the bark of a tree. A packing box of the proper size can, by the exercise of a little ingenuity, be turned into an acceptable rock.

Estimating Material

The amateur producing group that does not use care in purchasing lumber will soon find that their bills for this material are far over reaching the box-office receipts. Lumber should be cut with a very minimum of waste, and to that end, should be properly ordered from the yards.

Another study of Fig. 7 will repay the person about to order a bill of lumber. It will be noted that the scenery is twelve feet high. The stiles should therefore be cut from twelve feet pieces of lumber for most economy. Rails and toggle bars are six feet long or approximately six feet long.

Two of either can be cut from other twelve-foot pieces. By counting the number of equal length pieces to be used in a setting, the lumber can be ordered with the prospect of very little waste. A *cutting schedule*, showing exactly where each piece is to be used, should be retained to avoid mistakes in the scene shop. Lumber used in scene building comes in lengths of eight, ten, twelve, fourteen, sixteen and eighteen feet. By figuring all cuts from the proper length piece, maximum economy can be obtained.

Cloth is ordered on much the same system. A flat six feet wide by twelve feet high can be estimated as two yards wide by four yards high. It will therefore require eight square yards of material to cover the flat, or four yards of 72 inch material, or eight yards of 36 inch material. The total yardage of each flat can be added to obtain the bill of material for an entire setting.

The veneer for corner blocks and keystones can be estimated on much the same basis. In fact, the entire bill for scenery can and should be estimated down to the last nail and screw. A little forethought in this respect guarantees the financial solvency of the amateur producing group over a longer period of time.

Chapter II

SCENE PAINTING

No volume as compact as this can hope to explain the entire theory of color nor all the methods of handling it. This knowledge should preface any original attempt at the art of scene painting. All that can be accomplished in these limited pages are a few observations on general practice and a few specific answers to specific problems. Anyone desiring to gain a comprehensive understanding of color theory should read one of the several very excellent standard textbooks on the subject.

The Prang System

A study of the Prang System of color will be found very useful by the beginning scenic artist. There are three *primary colors,* red, blue and yellow. A primary color is a color which cannot be obtained by mixing any other colors. *Secondary colors* are obtained by mixing two primary colors. They are green (yellow and blue), orange (yellow and red), and violet or purple (red and blue). *Intermediate colors* result from the mixture of a primary and a secondary; yellow-green, blue-green, blue-violet, red-violet, red-orange, and yellow-orange.

The colors of the Prang System are combined into *harmonies* according to very definite rules. A harmony results when colors are combined for the most pleasing effect. First of all, there are the *complementary harmonies.* These are colors directly opposed to each other on the color chart; yellow and violet, orange and blue, yellow-orange and blue-violet, to name a few. A variation of this harmony is known as the *split complement.* A split comple-

ment includes both colors on each side of a direct complement as yellow and red-violet, violet and blue-violet. A
double split complement would include also the two colors
adjacent to yellow, yellow-orange and yellow-green. There
are also harmonies of *triads* or three colors. The three primary colors constitute the *primary triad* while the three
secondary colors form the *secondary* or *binary triad*. Intermediate colors such as blue-green, yellow-orange, and
red-violet may also form a color triad. *Analogous harmonies*
are composed of colors which are similar as red, red-violet,
and red-orange. Colors in any one of these harmonies may
be combined without *clashing*. A study of the chart will
disclose how other colors may be combined into harmonies
by following these same systems.

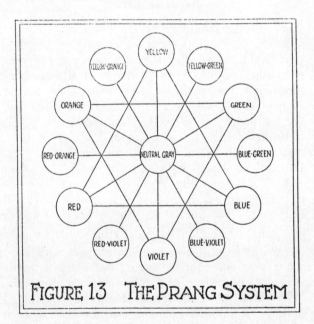

FIGURE 13   THE PRANG SYSTEM

A color is *neutralized* by mixing it with its complement.
Orange mixed with blue will produce a blue-gray and vice
versa. Two complements when mixed in nearly equal pro-

portions will produce neutral gray. In any single color harmony, most colors are neutralized while only one is left near its full *intensity* as an *accent*.

The *value* of a color is its lightness or darkness, its relation to black or white. A deep, dark blue is *low* in value while a very light blue is said to be *high* in value. Cobalt blue is higher in value than ultramarine blue.

These are only the basic rules of color and color harmony. A working knowledge of color should be obtained through study of both the Prang and Munsell Systems of color before any great amount of scene painting or stage designing is attempted.

Equipment

The tools of the scenic artist are few and fairly reasonable in price. Regulation brushes especially designed for scene painting are best, but they are more expensive. Expensive brushes have a strange habit of disappearing on most amateur stages at the moment when they are needed most. A few well chosen but more inexpensive brushes will serve the purpose just as well. Four sizes are necessary, a one-half inch brush for *striping* and *lining,* a four-inch brush and six-inch brush for general purpose and foliage painting, and a large kalsomining brush for *priming.* Brushes with short, stubby bristles are worse than useless. Even if a cheaper brush is chosen it should have bristles capable of painting a fine, sharp line when they are drawn to point on the edge of the paint pail.

The scenic artist will also provide himself with a box of colored chalk or charcoal for *laying out* work, a yardstick, and a straight-edge piece of light moulding about six feet long. The latter is used for drawing or painting long, straight lines. A moulding can usually be held against the canvas in such a way that an outside edge does not touch the canvas. This results in the elimination of blots and smears as a *loaded* brush is run along the edge in drawing a straight line. On very large pieces of scenery, drops, or wings hinged together as flats, a carpenter's *snap line* and blue chalk are used for laying out long, straight lines.

Mixing Paint

Colors: Stage scenery is painted with *dry color* mixed with water and glue. These colors are available in great variety, but those most used are the following:

Chrome Yellow (Light)	Cobalt or Italian Blue
Golden Ochre	Chrome Green
Chrome Orange	(Medium)
(Medium)	Burnt Umber
American Vermilion	Van Dyke Brown
Parrot Red	Swedish Black
Venetian Red	French, Belgian, or
Ultramarine Blue	Spanish Whiting

Almost any tint or shade of any color can be mixed from the above, but, on occasion, some shade will be required that can only be approached by using one of the more expensive colors. However, for most general purpose work, the above colors are sufficient and satisfactory.

Mixing: The best plan is to mix dry color to the required tint or shade before the water is added. In the original powdered state, color will give a very close approximation of its final appearance when dry. After the color has been thoroughly stirred, results can be checked by rubbing a pinch or two on a piece of white cardboard or canvas with the thumb.

Assume that a rather light and *neutral* (grayed) shade of yellow-green is wanted. Enough whiting is poured into a pail to cover the scenery to be painted. A safe margin will be about two pounds for every one hundred square feet. Enough chrome green is added to nearly approach the tint desired, stirring constantly while the color is added. Afterwards, the yellow is added, then a small quantity of red or vermilion, the *complement* of green, to *neutralize* the whole. The mixture is stirred constantly during the addition of any color. Results can be seen in this manner and less color is wasted. When the tint is satisfactory, enough water is added to bring the mixture to the consistency of very light cream. The color should flow freely from the brush and at the same time cover the surface with an even coat of color.

Glue: Glue or *sizing* is added to water color paint to make it stick to the canvas. *Ground* or *flaked gelatine glue* is dissolved in water by heating it over a stove or hot plate in a double boiler arrangement of pails. This is necessary to keep the glue from burning. The odor of burnt glue is one of the most disagreeable in the world and should be avoided if the dignity of the scene painting department is to be maintained. Enough water should be kept in the glue and it should be kept hot enough to flow easily from the pail when poured. Glue that is too cold or heavy becomes stringy in the paint. Each gallon of paint will require about one and one-half cups of melted glue. If not enough glue is used, the paint will powder and rub from the canvas when it is dry. If too much is used, the glue *crystallizes* in little, bright flakes on the canvas and spoils the purity and even tone of the color. Experience is the best teacher in this respect.

The Painter at Work

The first discovery of the beginner who approaches scene painting in any serious sort of way will be the fact that he cannot be hesitant about it. Everything must be painted with sufficient freedom and force to *carry* to the farthest rows of the auditorium. This is called *projection,* and it cannot be obtained by the frightened little soul who is afraid to paint with vigor. If there is any question about the perfection of a finished piece of work before beginning, a trial heat should be run off on an old and discarded piece of scenry. This will prevent the marks of indecision from ruining the finished painting.

Neither should paint be applied without some regard for the color of the costumes to be worn against the painted background or the predominant colors in the lighting. These considerations are all of major importance and come properly under the head of design. They should be considered carefully before the paint is applied. Forethought in this respect will avoid much future disappointment.

Priming: Raw or unpainted scenery is *primed* before any color is applied. A light, neutral coat of paint containing a slightly larger amount of glue is applied first. The priming coat fills the pores of the cloth and gives a smoother, more substantial surface on which to work. It must be admitted, however, that scenic artists frequently combine the painting of the prime coat and the *base coat* into one operation. The base coat is the first or general tone of the setting or individual piece of scenery. There can be no objection to this practice provided that the base coat is heavy enough to make the scenery *light proof*, that is, disconcerting shadows of toggle bars do not appear through the setting should a stray light happen to be turned on backstage. It is more desirable to prime all drops and borders before painting. An evenly applied coat of prime will give these pieces a much longer life and will add appreciably to their appearance.

Broken Surfaces: Plain, flat, and unbroken colors appear dull and uninteresting when shown on the stage. *A broken surface* is used to avoid this state of affairs. Broken surfaces are achieved by adding small areas of *contrasting* or *analogous* colors to the base coat. When this is properly done, the colors come to life, are said to "dance." There is a variety of methods by which this effect can be obtained.

Spattering: The most common broken surface is one which has been spattered. Tiny drops of paint are thrown on the canvas by giving a fairly dry brush a smart flick with the wrist. The painter stands at some distance from his work and literally throws the color on the surface, although spattering can be done by hitting the brush against the side of the left hand while standing only a foot or so from the work. The object is to make the spatter appear as smooth and even as possible. Too much paint on the brush should be avoided. The secret of successful spattering is to load the brush each time with nearly equal quantities of paint. Unless it is desired to make a rough looking surface, it is safer to keep the drops of paint as small as possible.

Very rarely will only one color be used in spattering. Two or more colors are usually superimposed one upon the other. This juxtaposition of specks of color upon a painted surface is governed by a system known as the *pointillage theory* of color. In other words, a succession of fine dots of yellow and blue in nearly equal quantities will, at a distance, combine to produce the effect of green. More yellow dots than blue will produce yellow-green, more blue dots will produce blue-green and so on through the entire spectrum of colors. A combination of the three primary colors, red, blue, and yellow, will produce a neutral gray.

The advantages of such a system are obvious. Color, instead of being flat and dull, achieves a scintillating life. The tone of the setting can be changed through the use of color in light. Blue light will accentuate the blue dots, amber the yellow, and magenta or red light the red dots. The whole system is designed to give the maximum amount of flexibility and texture to a painted surface. To make any great degree of difference in the tonality of a setting through the use of lights, the dots of color on the scenery must be very fine and even and very close together.

Spattered colors are applied over a base coat in a neutral shade of the final color desired. If green is to be the finished color, the base coat will be a flat, neutral green tone.

Stippling: Stippling is done with a sponge. One side of the sponge is trimmed off with a pair of scissors until it has a flat surface. The sponge is charged with color (not too much) and patted lightly over the surface to be broken. The job must be done evenly. The sponging should not show sudden, heavy blotches of color that mar the texture of the surface. It is well to keep patting the sponge in an even succession of circular or spiral motions to avoid noticeable changes in the pattern of the stippling. Stippling is used to indicate the rough plaster surfaces of walls. On an interior setting it, of course, may be used in the same manner that stippling is done inside a house.

Rolling: Very interesting and unusual effects can be created through the medium of rolling. A piece of old burlap about eighteen inches square is frayed at the edges,

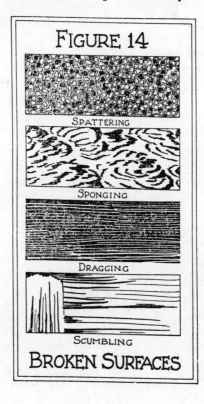

FIGURE 14

SPATTERING

SPONGING

DRAGGING

SCUMBLING

BROKEN SURFACES

dipped in paint, wrung out, and rolled evenly over the surface. There is no better method of indicating rough plaster or adobe exterior walls. One color may be effectively rolled over another as is done in spattering.

Dragging: Dragging is done with a nearly dry brush. The bristles are passed very lightly over the surface, leaving a succession of very fine hair-like lines. Dragging is used to indicate light shadows and especially the grain of weather-beaten wood or wood with a finished surface.

Naturally, the color of wood will vary according to the harmony of the setting, but brown is most frequent. To secure a rich, lustrous effect in this color, the base coat should be *laid in* with rather heavy burnt umber or Van Dyke brown. A somewhat neutral yellow-orange is first dragged very lightly over the base coat. A rich but neutral shade of red-violet is then dragged over the yellow-orange. Respectively, lighter and darker shades of these two colors may be used for outlining the highlights and shadows of mouldings or other architectural features in the wood. The best policy is to drag the darker color over the lighter one. In fact, this is the best method of handling broken colors of any kind.

Scumbling: Scumbling is similar to dragging except that the brush is loaded with a larger amount of color. Scumbling is used to advantage in painting rough stone work or rocks and heavy, broken, or pitted plaster. In practice, lighter colors are scumbled over a dark base coat. It may be done with good effect over an old paint job that is dark in color without other preparation. For instance, a shade of light cream or buff may be scumbled over a dark blue-gray to represent a rough plaster wall. In work of this kind, the direction of the brush strokes is altered frequently from an up and down to a cross-wise direction as the work proceeds.

Rocks are painted by scumbling. A dark blue-gray may be used for the base coat while the highlights and shadows are represented by two contrasting shades of another color.

Rocks must be painted boldly. They are indicated on a flat surface by scumbling each side of single rocks in a different direction. Irregularities in texture are made by giving the brush a slight twist with the wrist as it moves along.

Floating or *Blending:* This process is not always recognized as a broken surface, but it has its uses in relieving the monotony of large areas of flat color. Dark and light areas are filled in with their proper colors, and then, while the paint is still wet, a brush is passed over the entire surface in long, smooth strokes, blending or "floating" the two colors together. The method is not recommended until considerable skill has been acquired in the handling of scene paint. Much the same effect can be accomplished to a minor degree after the paint is dry by dipping a wide brush in warm water and sweeping it over the work. At no time should the color be "scrubbed" when such blending is done.

Glazing: Glazing is done to accentuate or mellow colors in small areas. It is a process of laying a transparent wash of one color over another. The color is thinned out with a very weak solution of melted glue and then washed lightly over the surface with a brush. The color underneath must not be disturbed.

Liquid or *crystal dye* may be used for the same purpose. It is mixed with water according to the directions of the manufacturer and applied with a brush. Dye is difficult for the novice to handle. Mistakes are all but impossible to correct without doing a great deal of the work over again.

Discretion must be used in breaking surfaces. If two, three, or even four colors are used, they must be chosen to harmonize. Nor is it advisable to break surfaces evenly. This is especially true of large, flat areas uninterrupted by doors, windows, or architectural decorations. The wall surface of an interior setting is shaded carefully into areas of both light and dark colors. This may be accomplished in two ways. The spattering or dragging may not be as heavy in the light areas, or if two colors are used, a light and a dark, the lighter color will predominate in the light areas.

FIGURE 15   LIGHT AND SHADOW

The human eye naturally travels toward light. Since this is true, the lighter areas must of necessity be more intense near the psychological center of the setting. This is, of course, the center of attention as applied to the actors and the story they are telling. Unless this is done, there will be opposing centers of interest on the stage to the confusion of any unified interest in the play on the part of the audience. The top and upstage corners of the setting will be the darkest of all while the lightest areas will be somewhere near the eye level line of the audience. A more artistic effect will result if darker colors are also shaded into doors, windows, and fireplaces. It helps bind these features into the stage picture. The proper method of distributing light and shadow in the painting of an interior setting is illustrated in Fig. 15. It will be noted that the light areas take into account the position of the furniture and combine to form a sort of "light arch" across the entire setting. When stage lighting and painting combine in a simple interior to produce this effect, light and shadow may be said to be properly considered.

The Interior Setting

The two following suggestions for interior settings are not offered as superb examples of the scene painter's art but rather as two serviceable settings which may be used for a variety of modern domestic comedies. Neither of them is beyond the efforts of the tyro, and yet, both may be painted to look as well as the best professional setting.

The Stenciled Setting: The color scheme of this setting embraces a split complement, red and green with blue-green and yellow-green. The work may be conveniently divided into three stages.

First Stage: The base coat is a very light tint of yellow-green. Over this is applied a spatter of red and blue-green. The red is slightly neutralized and quite high in value, *i.e.*, very light, almost a pink. The blue-green is a trifle darker in shade and is neutralized until it approaches an olive-green. Both colors are spattered lightly. The blue-green is spattered heaviest toward the top of the setting. It is not necessary to spatter the top border and baseboard of the setting. On a twelve-foot setting, the top border should be fourteen inches wide and the baseboard ten inches wide. To avoid spattering these sections, a sheet of newspaper or compo-board may be laid over them. Care should be taken to make the spatter even and have it flow nicely into the shaded areas at the top.

Second Stage: This is the stenciling. Stenciling is a long, tedious job, but there is nothing difficult about it. There are several little tricks which will appreciably speed up a job of stenciling.

Stencils are cut from oiled *stencil paper* especially made for the purpose. It is possible to procure at a slightly lower price a stencil paper which has not been oiled, but it is necessary to rub this paper thoroughly with linseed oil before it can be used for scenery. The wet paint will otherwise cause the stencil to fall apart before the setting is completed.

Two things must be borne in mind when making a stencil for an all-over design (Fig 16). First, it must present a more or less solid mat of color when the job is completed. There must be no great, attention compelling, solid masses of color. They must be broken up into small areas. The stenciled design must form merely a background and not call attention to itself. Second, it is advisable, if possible, to make the design to some unit of measurement that will conveniently fit all the flats. A design thirteen and three-quarter inches square is certain to cause trouble when it comes time to match up the edges of the flats.

Tiny *guide holes* are cut in each corner of the design. By tacking a light stick across the flat, it is only necessary to match the guide holes each time the stencil is moved. This prevents any erratic wandering of the design over the setting. The best method is to lay two flats together when it comes time to stencil over the joints. The use of tiny guide holes for the purpose of matching the design will never be apparent in the finished work.

The stenciling is done in two colors with a short, round *stenciling brush.* The stems and leaves are of a green somewhat brighter than that used in the spattering. It should be a sharper green and yet possess a certain effect of mossiness. Red is used for the flower and the bud, a red that is quite light and somewhat neutral. If, after the stenciling is done, the design appears too sharp, it may be necessary to again spatter over the top of the design. The purpose of the spatter is to prevent the design from standing out too boldly.

It will be found more convenient to make a light, wooden frame for the stencil for ease in handling. Also, the stencil should be thoroughly wiped off each time it is laid away. A flat weight placed on the stencil will prevent the cut edges of the design from curling disastrously and spoiling future work.

Third Stage: The third stage has to do with finishing off the border and the baseboard. The top border is of the same general tone as the base coat. A bit more yellow is added to the base coat and dragged very lightly over the border. It will be noted that the dragging is done in an up and down direction. This has a tendency to make the setting appear higher. If interior borders or a ceiling are used with the setting, they should be painted the color of the border.

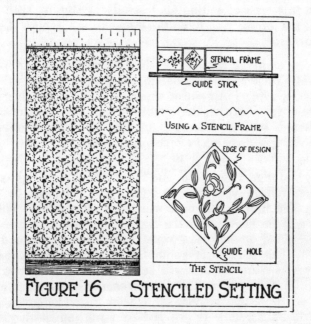

FIGURE 16   STENCILED SETTING

The baseboard is painted of the same green as the stencil except that it should be a trifle heavier in tone. The baseboard is dragged in a horizontal direction with a slightly more neutralized color of the same shade as that used in dragging the border.

The mouldings are painted of the same color as the baseboard. They are *lined* at the top edge with a thin line of the color used in dragging the baseboard, and on the bottom, with a very deep blue-green. A little shadow may be added under each moulding by lightly dragging with the same blue-green.

The doors and window frames are painted in the same manner and in the same color as the mouldings.

This type of setting will, of course, not do for an ultramodern interior, but it will have a wide use in mounting those myriads of plays which take place in the typical home of small American villages and cities. The author has used this type of setting successfully in staging such plays as *Wind in the South, Little Women,* and *Mother Carey's Chickens.*

The Spattered Setting: A useful type of setting for the average amateur stage is one that will work with equal facility as a typical American interior or as a suitable background for more modern furniture and decorations. The spattered setting described in the following paragraphs answers this demand as much as possible.

The color scheme is based on an intermediate triad of yellow-orange, blue-green, and red-violet. A very light slightly neutralized yellow-orange (buff) is used for the base coat. The first spatter coat will be of pure yellow. The yellow will be heaviest in the lighter portions of the setting. The second spatter is a very moderately neutralized red-violet. The red-violet should be near the color popularly known as Burgundy. It will be heaviest in the darker portions of the setting. The little stenciled decoration at the top of the setting is done in a deep, rich blue-green while a little light yellow is dragged over the top border in the manner previously described.

The base color of the mouldings and the baseboard is a rich burnt umber or Van Dyke brown. They are dragged in two colors: first, a slightly neutralized yellow-orange, and second, the same red-violet which was used for the spatter. A thin line of yellow is drawn at the top of each moulding and a thin line of blue-violet at the bottom to indicate the light and shadow of these pieces.

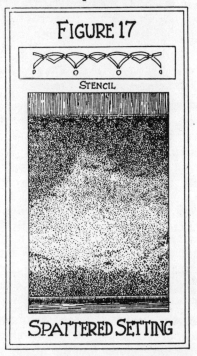

Panels: As a general rule, painted panels are not used in modern staging. Painted shadows are anathema to the modern designer. He prefers to build panels in their full relief, but there are occasions when due to cost or other factors a slavish attempt at reconstructing architectural forms is impractical.

Fig. 18 shows the method of painting a simple panel. The grain of the wood in each portion is indicated by changing the direction of the dragging. Light and shadow are indicated with appropriate colors. It is important that all

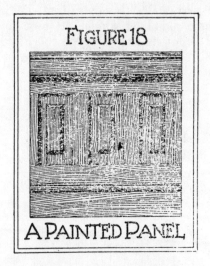

lines drawn when painting a panel be sharp and clear. They must not appear to have been painted "with the stub end of a cat tail."

Ordinarily, wood is painted in the colors recommended for the baseboard of the spattered setting mentioned previously, but if the color scheme of the setting demands it, there is no artistic reason why the woodwork should not be painted blue or any other color. In these cases, it is necessary to choose colors for the dragging which are naturally harmonious with the base coat selected.

It may be well to mention that doors and windows on the stage are frequently painted in oil colors, but there is really no justification for this practice. Scene paint can be applied to wood if care is taken to see that it possesses enough glue or sizing. A glossy looking door or window is very obvious in a setting painted in the flat colors of scene paint and reminds one of nothing so much as some of the peculiar staging seen in a third rate stock company.

The Exterior Setting

The best judgment of the scenic artist is demanded in the painting of an exterior setting. In the old days, scenic artists painted woodland scenes with such an overpowering assortment of plants and vines that it appeared as if God in his wisdom had seen fit to endow even our sparse northern forests with all the wild profusion of a tropical jungle. Designers today try to make exterior scenes as simple and as tasteful as possible. A few solid looking tree trunks and a draped border to represent the foliage are all that are frequently used, but tree trunks and foliage can be successfully painted if a little reticence and discretion is practiced.

Tree Trunks: In painting the trunk of a tree on a wood-wing or other flat surface, two things are of primary importance, the roundness of the tree and the texture of the bark. The colors may be based on either a scheme of brown or gray, but brown appears the richer of the two under the usual lighting of the stage. The trunk is first laid in with an even coat of burnt umber to which a little red and yellow or orange has been added. Shadows on each side of the trunk to give the feeling of roundness are next filled in by adding a little ultramarine blue and vermilion to the brown. Shadows should be rather violet in tone. On top of the violet and fading toward the center, a higher and somewhat redder variant of the base coat is used. The center or highlighted portions of the trunk are laid in with a neutralized orange.

A wide variety of colors may be used in painting tree trunks. The important thing is the texture of the brush strokes. Each color is applied with short, clean strokes of the brush and each color fades into the one adjacent. A portion of the original brown should always show through between the strokes. The colors should be kept as rough as possible. If it is necessary to smoothen the appearance of the tree any, this may be done after the paint is dry by dipping a brush in warm water and blending the colors

FIRST STEP

BLUE-GREEN

YELLOW-GREEN

SECOND STEP

THIRD STEP

THREE STEPS IN PAINTING FOLIAGE

NEUTRAL ORANGE

REDDISH BROWN

BLUE VIOLET

PALM TREES

A TREE TRUNK

FIGURE 19   TREES AND FOLIAGE

a bit more together. If the trunk appears too flat, a little light yellow may be touched in here and there to accent the highlights. Fig. 19 indicates the distribution of color and the character of the brush strokes used in painting a tree.

Foliage: There should be no attempt made to paint individual leaves. Masses of foliage are the important consideration. Except for the two first base coats, the color is applied in short, quick strokes of the brush. The brush is given a quick twist with the wrist each time to impart a leafy character to the stroke. The trick is acquired with a little practice.

At least six colors are required to successfully indicate foliage, a very deep blue-green, a lighter and more brilliant blue-green, two shades of yellow-green, one more yellowish in tone and the other more green, a shade of pure, slightly neutralized green, and red-violet.

A base coat of the deep blue-green is applied first. Masses of this color are then roughly outlined by using the yellow yellow-green as in the first stage of Fig. 19. Both are painted in roughly but in solid colors. The shady portions of each mass of leaves are then touched in with the lighter blue-green, using the short, quick strokes mentioned previously (Second Stage). A few strokes of the red-violet are then touched in here and there over the entire surface. After this, the main portions of each mass of leaves are laid in with the neutralized green, always allowing some of the colors underneath to show through. The highlights are then applied with the greenish yellow-green. (Fig. 19).

Most important of all, foliage should not be painted in any stiff or constrained manner. A large brush should be used and handled in such a manner that it covers the surface rapidly and surely with swift, free strokes. Minor masses of foliage such as small brushes and trees are painted in the same manner except on a smaller scale.

Ground Rows: Scenic pieces that are presumably a much greater distance from the eyes of the audience than the immediate foreground of the setting are painted in lighter colors. It is safer not to paint such pieces with too much minor detail. A few large masses of appropriate color blended together and broken here and there by distant trees and breaks in the terrain, all touched in very roughly, makes the best method of painting such pieces.

Palm Trees: Occasionally an operetta or similar production requires the use of palm trees and more tropical appearing foliage. These are easily painted. A broad single line is first applied over the light brown of the base coat for the highlighting of the trunks. A darker brown is used for indicating the markings that distinguish this type of tree. In the foliage, each leafy "fan" is painted in a single shade of green. These individual fans are painted one over the other until the entire mass of palm fronds has been completed. Tropical foliage along the ground may be indicated with the same long, sweeping strokes of the brush (Fig. 19).

Successful scene painting comes through practice and a continuous search for ideas. The various women's magazines are filled with illustrations of tasteful interiors that can many times be worked into excellent stage settings. Posters and travel literature of various kinds are fine sources of inspiration for the artist who must paint a characteristic scene. A greedy search for ideas develops the embryo scenic artist. A large scrapbook into which pictures can be pasted and notes written is a worthwhile acquisition.

Chapter III

STAGE LIGHTING

The function of stage lighting may be classified under two main divisions: first, *illumination*, and second, *interpretation*. The first concerns itself solely with *visibility*. It requires only that we be able to see the actors and the setting. The problems of interpretation are broader in scope and embrace such considerations as color, the time of day or season of the year, and the emotional or psychological content of the play itself. These divisions in the field of stage lighting are merely for the purpose of analysis. In a well lighted production, the two elements are part of an artistic and unified whole.

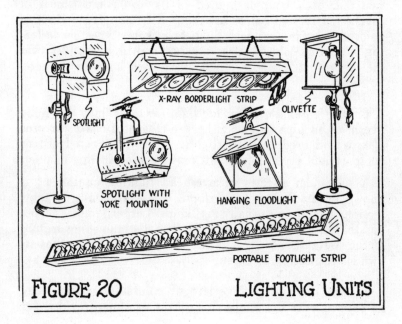

FIGURE 20   LIGHTING UNITS

Equipment

The mechanics of stage lighting are first concerned with *general illumination*, and second, with *specific illumination*. General illumination is primarily a problem in visibility and is obtained through the use of three types of equipment, *footlights, borderlights*, and *floodlights*.

Footlights: There are two types of footlights, the *open faced type* and the *compartment type*. Footlights are usually just a metal trough with 50 or 60 watt *lamps* (bulbs) spaced at intervals of six or eight inches across the bottom. To obtain various colors, the lamps are either *dipped* in *lamp dye* or have the color blown directly into the glass when the lamp is made. The latter are called *natural colored lamps* and may be obtained in either red, green, amber, or blue.

Compartment type footlights are distinguished by the fact that each lamp is *housed* in its own compartment or division. Different colors are secured by slipping a sheet of colored *gelatine* over each light, or in some types, by fastening a round, colored glass *medium* called a *roundel* over the individual reflector which backs each lamp in the footlights.

Borderlights: Portable footlight sections may be hung overhead on pipe battens either by means of chains or *pipe clamps* and used as borderlights. Either the open faced or compartment type of footlight may be used in this manner.

A particular species of overhead lighting equipment is known as the *X-Ray borderlight*. These are built in short sections containing usually six lamps. Larger lamps of from 250 to 300 watts rating are used. The distinguishing feature of the X-Ray borderlight is the fact that each lamp has its own spun glass or metal reflector.

Frames containing a variety of colors in gelatine may be slipped over the lamps in grooves or slots provided for the purpose. Any number of such sections of X-Ray border-lights may be hung overhead on a single batten. The first borderlight downstage, the one located immediately behind the grand drapery, is called the *concert border*. In modern lighting practice, it is frequently the only borderlight used.

Floodlights: Floodlights or *olivettes* are large tin boxes containing a lamp of high wattage (1000 to 2000 watts) and are used for flooding particular areas with light. They may *work* from a *stand* resting on the floor or may be hung overhead on a batten. A smaller type of floodlight shaped similar to the one in Fig. 20 is sometimes referred to as a *pan*.

Spotlights: Specific illumination is provided by spot-lights. There is the greatest variation in this most useful piece of stage lighting equipment. It includes small *baby spots* of from 250 to 400 watts capacity up to huge arc spotlights requiring several amperes of current. The ama-teur technician working on a small stage will find that the 400 or 500 watt spotlight will be his most useful piece of equipment. On occasion, a 1000 watt spotlight will be neces-sary, but the smaller types will serve the purposes of most dramatic production.

Control

To be practical for the stage, there must be some cen-tralized system for controlling the quantity and distribution of current to the several pieces of equipment. This is the function of the *switchboard*. The switchboard contains switches for turning the lights on and off and *dimmers* for regulating the amount of current flowing to any piece of equipment.

Switchboard installations may be wired for either *per-manent* or *flexible* control of the lighting units. Most stages are already wired permanently with a switchboard or *panel board* of some kind. It is not wise for the amateur to dis-turb this wiring without having the work done by a licensed electrician. However, if an *outlet* for additional current is available, there is no reason why the stage technician should not use it for as many pieces of extra equipment as are desirable. For maximum efficiency, this current may be handled through flexible control.

Flexible control consists in wiring a switchboard so that any number of lighting units, floodlights or spotlights, may be operated on a single switch or dimmer at various times throughout the course of a performance. The method cuts down the number of dimmers required to operate a show and as a result makes possible the proper handling of lights with the very minimum of these expensive pieces of equipment. Flexible control is accomplished by *plugging in* each lighting unit to the switch and dimmer circuit as it becomes necessary to use it. Fig. 21, showing the use of a salt water dimmer, diagrams how two lamps may be plugged into the dimmer circuit as the occasion demands. This is flexible control.

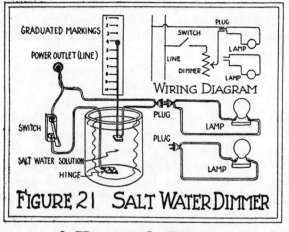

FIGURE 21   SALT WATER DIMMER

A Homemade Dimmer

Dimmers manufactured especially for the control of stage lighting are the best, but they are quite high in price. A salt water dimmer can be easily made at home. The operation of the dimmer is based on the *resistance* offered to the passage of an electrical current by a salt water solution. A large crock or glassware container (not metal) is filled with water and a handful of salt tossed in and thoroughly stirred. If it is not planned to use a larger lighting unit than the rated *capacity* of such wire, ordinary extension cord may be used for the wiring. A single strand of this double cord is soldered to a small hinge and placed in the bottom of the jar. Another single strand of the wire is soldered to another hinge or small piece of metal and tied to a short piece of rather heavy cord. The light is dimmed or brightened by raising or lowering the cord in the water. When the hinge on the cord is raised completely out of the solution, the light is out. When the two metal contacts touch each other on the bottom of the jar, the light burns at its full intensity. By attaching a small ring to the end of the cord and graduating a series of markings on a board by means of small nails, the dimmer can always be brought accurately to any predetermined state of intensity.

Homemade Lighting Equipment

Progressive amateur producing organizations should carefully budget a certain portion of their income for the purchase of new lighting equipment. Because this equipment is expensive, most organizations will find this a slow process. Homemade equipment, while possibly not as good, will serve until such time as finances permit more elaborate arrangements. Even moderately good lighting secured through the use of more or less makeshift equipment is to be preferred over no attempt at lighting.

Pails, pans, and the larger sizes of tin cans (the No. 10 size) can be made into acceptable pieces of lighting equipment if a little ingenuity is used. Fig. 22 illustrates some of these pieces.

Floodlights: Provision must be made first of all for the lamp. Porcelain *receptacles* will be found best for this pur-

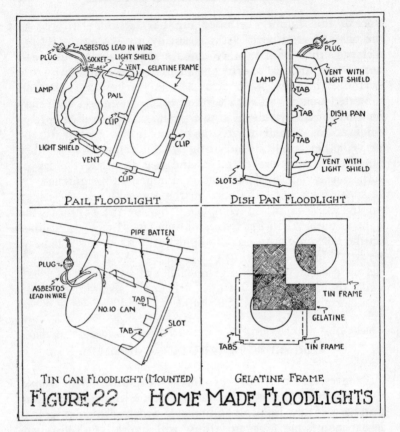

FIGURE 22   HOME MADE FLOODLIGHTS

pose. If a *G Type* (globular) lamp larger than 400 watts is used or a *PS Type* (pear shaped), it will be necessary to use the larger type of receptacle, the *mogul* size. Lamps of smaller wattages will burn in sockets of the size used in house lighting. It should be remembered that PS Type lamps larger than 1000 watts are made to burn in a *base up* position, while G Type lamps should not be turned more than 45 degrees from a *base down* position. The receptacles can be fastened to the *housing* with small *stove bolts*. If large lamps are used, it is safer to provide asbestos covered *lead in* wires for each unit as the head of the lamp may cause the rubber insulation on other types of wire to melt and result in a short circuit. It is necessary to use about fifteen inches of this wire. It terminates in a plug or slip pin connector to which the wire or *stage cable* can be attached.

Vents should be provided for the free circulation of air inside the lamp housing to prevent the unit from becoming too hot. These vents should provide for the access of cool air on the bottom of the housing and for the emmission of the hot air at the top. They are fitted with *shields* so that there is no possibility of *light spill* from the unit. Holes are cut in the lamp housing and pieces of tin are bent and soldered over the openings as shown in Fig. 22.

Each unit should be equipped with some means of attaching *gelatine frames*. These enable the operator to change the color of the light as required. The frames may be simply wired in place or tin clips or slots may be soldered in place for the purpose. The simplest method is to cut the front of the unit from a single piece of tin and solder it in place by means of little tabs as shown in Fig. 22.

A floodlight should be painted on the inside with a coat or two of white enamel. Enamel reflects a much greater percentage of light than other kinds of flat white paint and is remarkably heat resistant. The appearance of homemade lighting equipment is much improved if the outside of each unit is painted with one or two coats of pure black enamel.

Spotlights: The construction of spotlights is a bit more complicated because these pieces demand a reflector and a lens. The lens is of the *plano-convex type*. The smaller sized lenses may be obtained from a large flashlight or larger sizes may be purchased quite reasonably if more elaborate spotlights are contemplated. If the spotlight is made of sufficient size, the reflector from an old automobile headlight may be used quite effectively.

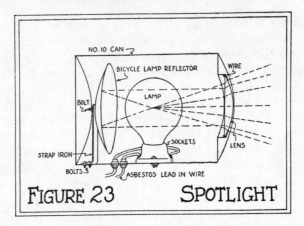

FIGURE 23   SPOTLIGHT

By the use of a little ingenuity, the one-gallon cans which contain varnish or linseed oil may be made into excellent pieces of lighting equipment. Several of these units are illustrated in Fig. 24.

Mountings: The use of homemade equipment presents one difficulty. Unless considerable work is done to make either *yoke* or *side mountings* for each piece, it is often impossible to make them hang without swinging at critical times and throwing the light where it is not wanted. This can be avoided usually by wiring them into place with light picture frame wire or stove pipe wire, but such an arrangement makes it difficult to change the direction of the light. A better job can be done by making a yoke mounting from a piece of light strap iron. By fastening this to the light housing with short *wing bolts*, the equipment can be tilted in any position desired. A radiator hose clamp such as is used in automobiles can be bolted to the top of the yoke mounting and used to clamp the unit to a pipe batten. Pipe flanges make a neat way of fastening floodlights to a pipe stand, but they have the disadvantage of swinging only in one direction. However, by also using a yoke mounting on floodlights and bolting these to the pipe flange, the difficulty can be overcome.

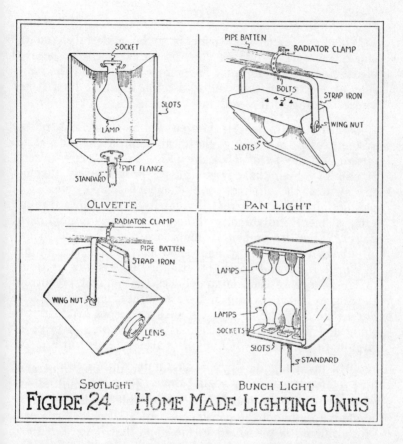

SOCKET

SLOTS

LAMP

PIPE FLANGE

STANDARD

OLIVETTE

PIPE BATTEN

RADIATOR CLAMP

BOLTS

STRAP IRON

WING NUT

SLOTS

PAN LIGHT

RADIATOR CLAMP

PIPE BATTEN

STRAP IRON

WING NUT

LENS

SPOTLIGHT

LAMPS

LAMPS

SOCKETS

SLOTS

STANDARD

BUNCH LIGHT

FIGURE 24   HOME MADE LIGHTING UNITS

Frames: Gelatine frames (Fig. 22) are easily made from two flat pieces of tin. One piece has little tabs around its outer edge which can be folded over the smaller piece. The round holes are cut in the tin by using either a pair of tin snips or a metal cutting saw. Gelatine frames are frequently made of cardboard with the edges pasted together by gummed tape, but the practice is rather dangerous as the cardboard may catch fire from the heat of the lamp.

Wiring

When any extensive wiring is to be undertaken on the stage, the work should be done by an experienced, licensed electrician, but there are a few simple facts about the handling of electricity that will assist the amateur to a better understanding of the equipment he uses.

Lighting equipment is *hooked up* in either one of the systems used in making electrical connections, the *series circuit*, or the *parallel circuit* (Fig. 25). A series circuit is one in which the current passes progressively through the switch, the dimmer, the element (lamp), etc. In a parallel circuit, the current divides itself and flows through each element individually though with no diminution of power. When a number of lamps are to be burned in one circuit they are usually connected in parallel as they are in borderlight and footlight circuits. Unless this is done, the resistance in each lamp reduces the amount of current flowing to the next lamp in a series circuit until all of them burn very dimly. Single lights, such as a spot or flood, are connected in series. The relationship of these two types of circuits to the main switchboard is also indicated in Fig. 25.

All control boards are not wired like the one illustrated in Fig. 25. Changes are made to reduce the multiplicity of wires behind the panel. It is inadvisable for the ordinary amateur to attempt the construction of a stage switchboard. This drawing is presented in the hope that it may dissolve the mystery which overhangs the stage switchboard in the mind of the amateur director or technician.

To wire these individual circuits on the stage to avoid the hazards of fire and burnt-out equipment, it is necessary to understand something of the primary rules which govern the control of electricity. The *volt* is the term used to designate the amount of electromotive force possessed by an electrical current. It corresponds to pressure in a water pipe line. For practical purposes, the ordinary 110 volt circuit will alone be considered. *Amperes* designate the rate of flow

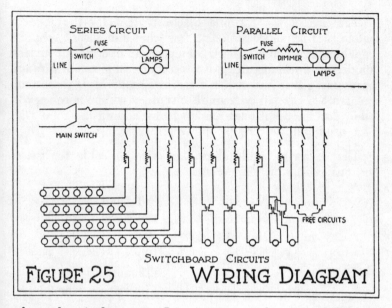

FIGURE 25   WIRING DIAGRAM

of an electrical current. It compares to the rate of flow in a water pipe, the number of gallons per minute. The *watt* is the unit of power and is equal to the volts multiplied by the amperes. It is expressed in the algebraic formula:

Watts=Volts x Amperes, or

$$W=VA$$

As a working basis, the amount of current (amperes) required to operate a 500 watt spotlight at 110 volts can be computed as follows:

VA=W, therefore

$$\frac{W}{V}=A$$

Stated in its numerical equivalents, the formula is

$$\frac{500}{110}=4.54$$

The figure, 4.54, is the number of amperes required to operate a 500 watt spotlight at 110 volts.

The use of the formula discovers that for the sake of safety, wiring and equipment (switches and fuses) must be capable of carrying at least 5 amperes to operate a 500 watt spotlight. It will require a No. 16 stage cable rated at 6 amperes and a fuse and switch rated at 5 amperes. If more than one lamp is carried on a single circuit, it will be necessary to allow for the additional amperage by adding the total wattage used and dividing by the volts.

The following table shows the size of cable to use at various ratings in amperes:

3 amps.—No. 18		50 amps.—No. 6	
6 amps.—No. 16		70 amps.—No. 4	
15 amps.—No. 14		90 amps.—No. 2	
20 amps.—No. 12		100 amps.—No. 1	
25 amps.—No. 10		125 amps.—No. 0	
35 amps.—No. 8		150 amps.—No. 00	

Dimmers: Dimmers are rated according to wattage. The 250-500 and 1100 watt sizes are most useful on the amateur stage. Care must be taken not to *overload* the rated capacity of any dimmer; for instance, attempt to dim a load of 1500 watts on a 1100 watt dimmer. Although most dimmers will carry more than their rated capacity, persistent overloading invariably results in burning out an expensive dimmer.

The above dimmers are of the *resistance type.* They vary the brightness of a lamp by offering a resistance to the amount of current flowing to the lamp. Recently, there has come into favor on small stages a dimmer of the auto-transformer type. These have the advantage of being small, inexpensive, and they do not heat as the resistance dimmers do. In addition, they have a completely variable capacity up to their maximum rating; that is, an auto-transformer type dimmer rated at 850 watts will completely dim any size lamp from five watts up to and including 850 watts. It will pay the purchaser of a small switchboard to investigate the advantages of this type dimmer.

Slip pin connectors are used for making connections on the stage. They take the place of the utility plugs used in house wiring. They are available in both five and fifteen ampere sizes, a range sufficient to cover most stage uses. The *stage plug* rated at 50 amperes is used for carrying heavier loads. There is a distinction to be observed in making connections with plugs or connectors. One side of the connection is called the *line*, the other the load. The line is the "live" side, the side which carries the current, while the load side is connected to the piece of equipment. The half of a connector with the two prongs is *always* connected to the side leading to the lamp and not to the live end of the wire. This prevents the possibility of short circuiting or shock by accidentally touching the two projecting prongs of the connector.

The use of makeshift equipment on the stage carries with it a certain danger from fire. It is best to use wire and connectors of the approved type and to be eternally vigilant in guarding against short circuits and worn places in the cable. Lighting units should be kept away from draperies or other inflammable materials. If they are attached directly to a wood batten, they should be insulated from the wood either with a sheet of asbestos or heavy tin. If wiring is done in the approved manner, there is, however, little danger of such an emergency as fire.

Color

Color in stage lighting is obtained by placing a *color medium*, over the source of light. A color medium may be either of glass, *gelatine*, *transolene*, or cellophane.

Gelatine: Gelatine is the most adaptable color medium for general stage use. It is available in a wide range of colors, is fairly cheap, and, if carefully handled, will last for a considerable time. Pieces of the size required are cut from the standard sheets measuring twenty by twenty-four inches. The sheets of gelatine are inserted in gelatine frames and placed over the lighting units in the manner previously detailed.

Transolene: Transolene is more resistant to heat and general wear and tear than is gelatine but is slightly higher in price. If gelatine is well cared for and packed away after each time it is used in a cardboard folder, it may be made to last as long as transolene.

Other Media: Cellophane may be used, but it is not recommended except in cases of emergency. The range of color is very restricted in cellophane.

Sheets of colored glass may be used for mediums but the possibility of breakage discourages their general utility for the stage. Colored glass of any thickness also has a tendency to "eat up" much of the light coming from a lamp.

Handling Color: Light colors may be mixed in different ways to obtain other colors just as pigments may be mixed. For most stage purposes, light colors are mixed in accordance with the *additive theory* of light. It is literally adding one color to another to produce a third color. The additive light primaries are red, green, and blue. When one of these colors is produced from a separate piece of equipment and combined with another primary, the third color is produced. Red light combines with blue to produce purple, blue with green to produce blue-green, while red and green combine to produce yellow. The combination of a primary and a secondary color (blue and yellow) produces white light as does a combination of the three primaries, red, green and blue. It is this tendency of colors to combine in the production of white light which gives rise to the system of *cross-spotting* which will be explained in the section devoted to lighting practice.

It will be noted at the beginning that colored light has a very decided effect on the color of both costumes and scenery. This tendency of light should be taken seriously into account when designing costumes and scenery. To a certain extent, the probable effect of colored light on any material can be foretold, but actual experimentation is the only way that guarantees definite results.

Lighting Practice

Formerly, it was only considered necessary that the audience be able to see the actors. The stage was flooded with light from borderlights and footlights to give a flat, monotonous, and decidedly uninteresting effect. This idea has given way to one which demands that there be only one point of maximum interest or visibility on the stage, and that stage lighting should seek to maintain the appearance of the actors in their naturally rounded or three dimensional form rather than flat figures on a single plane. The

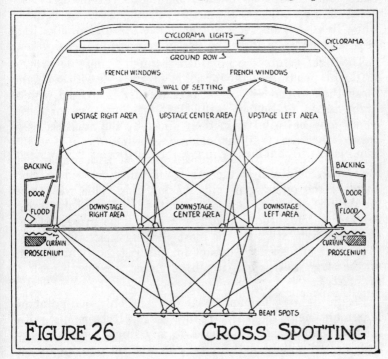

FIGURE 26   CROSS SPOTTING

growth of this idea has given birth to a system of *plastic* lighting for the stage.

Plastic lighting is based on cross-spotting. Although the system is capable of great variation according to the demands of the play or the limited availability of specified pieces of equipment, its operation can best be explained through a discussion of a nearly ideal arrangement (Fig. 26).

The stage is divided into a number of *light areas,* they are usually six or eight in number depending upon the size of the stage. Each of these areas is lighted by two converging spotlight beams. One beam is of a darker color while the other is of a lighter color, and they both combine to form white light. The effect is to leave one side of the actor's face and person in comparative shadow while the other side carries its natural highlights. From the viewpoint of the audience, the actor will appear to be in pure white light, but his face will not have the dull lifeless flatness which results from the use of pure white light.

The light colors are obtained through using the proper shade of gelatine. Daylight Blue is crossed with a Light Flesh Pink to produce white, or Lavender is crossed with a Light Straw, or Salmon with Daylight Blue. Any of these colors may be softened in their effect by the addition of a frosted medium over the colored gelatine.

To be consistent in the lighting plan, it is desirable that the darker colors always come from either one side of the stage or the other, generally the left side. This will place the darkest of the darker colors on the left side of the stage. A gradual and proper graduation should be preserved between the light areas for the most pleasing effect. Of course, if there is any specific reason for placing the lightest area on the stage down right, it can be placed there with perfect propriety.

Plastic lighting demands that there be only one point of maximum light intensity on the stage. It coincides with the most important acting area in any single scene. It may shift as the action of the play moves from one important area to another, but usually it is somewhere near center stage. To bring this area into proper relief, the remaining areas of the stage are dimmed to a proportionate low intensity. If, for instance, the spotlights used are of the 500 watt variety, it may be accomplished by hooking each pair of spotlights in each area to a single 1100 watt dimmer.

Ideally, the light beams from the spotlights should reach the stage at an angle somewhere near forty-five degrees. Spotlights on the concert border will serve very well to light the upstage areas, but effective lighting of the downstage areas usually means that spotlights must be placed somewhere in the auditorium. A false beam across the ceiling of the auditorium provides a masking for these spots so they are not seen by the audience. Spotlights so placed are known as *beam spots*.

The average amateur producing group does not possess sufficient equipment to light a production on the basis of the foregoing system. It means that compromises will have to be made, but if the operator uses his equipment to approximate as closely as possible the ideal arrangement, better and more artistic results can be created in stage lighting.

Special Effects

It should be borne in mind that colored light can be used with great effect to enhance the tone of flat pigments in the stage setting. Magenta may be used on the brown trunks of trees to enrich and intensify their coloring. Lights may be used to accent the folds in stage draperies, to soften them, or provide contrasts in their coloring. The possibilities along this line are so great that single suggestions would necessarily be endless. The conscientious lighting director will spend hours experimenting to perfect special effects in coloring.

Lights of some kind should be used behind all openings in the stage setting, behind doors and windows. A bunchlight, a pan, a short section of *striplights*, or an olivette may be used for this purpose. If the opening shows an exterior, Light Straw or Light Amber may be used to simulate sunlight, or a Light Blue Green or Moonlight Blue used to gain the effect of a night time.

The lighting of sky cycloramas requires special handling. Most amateur producers do not flood these pieces with sufficient light. The problem is to keep the light on the cyclorama as smooth and even as possible. The cyclorama should be lighted both from below and from above. There should be a greater intensity of light near the horizon than overhead. The effect may be accomplished by using a deeper blue (Urban Blue, Dark Blue) in the overhead lights and a lighter blue (Light Blue, Daylight Blue) in the lights on the floor.

There is no technical field in the threatre that will repay the experimentor with more personal satisfaction than lighting. As yet, the surface has only been scratched. The amateur producing group will do well to study seriously the technical side of stage lighting so that they may learn better how to control this element in achieving greater and more artistic results in the mounting of their plays.

Chapter IV

STAGE EFFECTS

A first rate dramatic production demands that all the offstage effects be as realistic as possible. No department of the theatre offers the stage technician a greater chance to display his ingenuity. Most sound effects can be created at home by mechanical means, but frequently it is cheaper to purchase more elaborate sound effects. Sound effects are recorded in great variety on regular records that may be played on a phonograph, although small, cheap models of these machines rarely give satisfactory results. Care must be taken to have the playing arm of the phonograph touch the needle to the record as lightly as possible, other wise the "surface scratch" of the record will be heard by the audience. Most good phonographs have a device for varying the weight of the playing arm on the record. A weight of three ounces will give the best results in most cases.

Thunder

This is one of the most easily accomplished of all stage effects. A piece of tin or light sheet metal is hung by ropes from the ceiling. The dimensions should be about three feet by six feet. The *thunder sheet* is more easily operated if a piece of light board is bolted to the bottom and a pair of handles provided. The effect of thunder is created by shaking the sheet either lightly or vigorously depending on the volume of thunder desired.

The effect of thunder can also be obtained by using a kettle drum, but this method is not as satisfactory as the one outlined above.

Rain

The sound of falling rain may be created in several ways. The simplest way is to place one or two handfuls of dried peas in the cover of a cardboard suit box and rattle them back and forth by hand.

Fig. 28 illustrates a more elaborate machine for securing the sound of falling rain. It is a wooden box with a tin bottom. By fastening the box to a pipe axle, it can be tilted back and forth to effectively rattle the peas. One or two light slats can be nailed across the bottom of the box on the inside to increase the rattling of the peas. The rain machine can also be used for securing the sound of beating surf by varying the rhythm in which the box is tilted.

There are occasions in plays when nothing but the actual fall of water outside of doors and windows will prove satisfactory. The effect is not as difficult as it sounds. A rubber hose is attached to a convenient faucet and brought on the stage. A piece of pipe in which numerous tiny holes have been bored is attached to the onstage end of the hose and hung overhead behind the doors and windows. As the water streams from the openings in the pipe, it falls into a light trough made of rubberized canvas and is carried off the stage through a hose. The beauty of the effect is enhanced by playing colored light on the falling drops of water.

Snow

Tiny scraps of white paper or confetti are best for the effect of falling snow. To work the effect, a stage hand climbs to the top of a stepladder with a dust pan full of these tiny particles. On the cue, he flicks them gently from the pan with a whisk broom. Like the rain effect, the appearance of the snow is improved if it is seen falling in a light blue light.

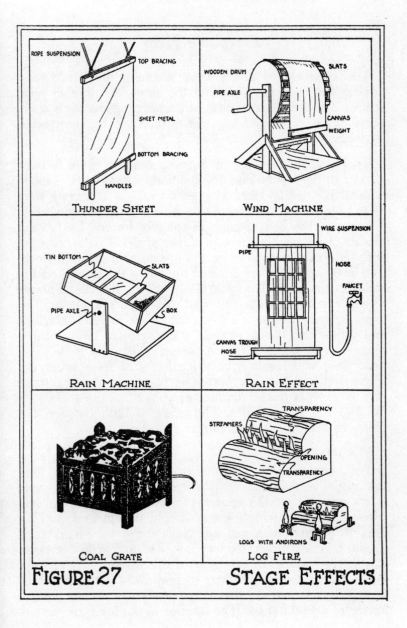

THUNDER SHEET

WIND MACHINE

RAIN MACHINE

RAIN EFFECT

COAL GRATE

LOG FIRE

FIGURE 27   STAGE EFFECTS

Fireplace Fires

The spectacle of a character warming his hands at a fireless fireplace has occurred too often in plays to need special comment here. Grates of burning logs or coals make some of the most pleasing effects that can be constructed by the amateur stage technician.

To simulate the effect of burning coals, a grate is built similar to the one in Fig. 28. The main frame work is made with 1"x2" white pine. The grill work in the grate may be cut out of either composition board or three-ply veneer. The top of the bed of coals is roughly formed by tacking chicken wire across the top of the grate. This is covered with light muslin as are also the openings in the grill work. The latter openings are covered by gluing the muslin on the inside of the grate. The general lines of the individual pieces of coal are marked out with black paint on the muslin. The areas in between the black markings are painted with red and yellow dye blended rather well together. Two or three electric light bulbs are then placed inside the grate. The best effect will result from using bulbs of from twenty to thirty watts. A *twinkle button* is placed in the socket of one bulb while *flasher buttons* are placed in the sockets of the two remaining bulbs. The effect of light between the pieces of coal in the grate is very realistic.

The effect of burning logs will require a little more time to build but is not at all difficult. The two individual logs are made very similar to the tree trunk previously outlined except that the center portion of each log is left transparent by pasting a piece of light muslin over it. This area is painted with red and yellow dye. A small crack should be left between the two logs. Red and yellow streams of silk are fastened to each side of this opening. An electric fan is placed behind the logs to keep these little streamers fluttering in a manner that very closely approaches the behavior of actual flames. The interior of the log construction is lighted with three low wattage bulbs exactly as outlined in the construction of the coal grate.

If smoke is desired in the fireplace, it can be obtained by hanging bits of very thin grey gauze from the top of the inside of the fireplace opening. As these pieces are waved gently back and forth by an electric fan, they resemble smoke.

Horses' Hoofs

The classic method of imitating the sound of horses' hoofs on the stage is through the use of two halves of a cocoanut shell. The halves are grasped in the hands of the operator and struck smartly on a board or table. A little practice is necessary to obtain the correct rhythm. If it is desired to have the beating of the hoofs sound on soft earth, the tale or board must be padded with several thicknesses of burlap sacking or other heavy cloth material.

Lightning

The effect of lightning may be obtained by causing an electric arc to jump between a piece of steel and a piece of carbon, but it is much simpler to employ one of the photoflood lamps used in photography. These give an intense white light very similar to lightning. For best results, the lamps should be mounted in a floodlight and operated with a switch that can be easily snapped on and off to give the effect of intermittent flashes of lightning.

Jagged gashes of chain lightning can be produced by covering the floodlight with a cardboard shield into which the outline of the lightning flash has been cut. The floodlight is placed in such a fashion that the image is cast upon the sky cyclorama.

Door Slam

If a spare door is available, it should be braced up offstage to give the effect of a door slam. Lacking this, an artificial slam can be created by using a piece of plank about three feet long and a length of sash cord or light manila rope. The rope is fastened to one end of the plank by using a heavy screw eye. The operator holds the rope in his hand and has one foot on the plank which is raised slightly above the floor. On the cue, he drops the plank smartly to the floor. Offstage door slams should be kept in the character of the person who has just left the stage. A dignified old gentleman does not slam a door like a boisterous young school boy.

Bells and Buzzers

For the sake of convenience, door bells and buzzers are usually mounted in one neat little box which may be carried anywhere about the stage as needed. A piece of light strap iron screwed to the back of the box and bent into the shape of a hook facilitates hanging the whole apparatus on the toggle bars of the settings.

Door bells and buzzers are connected exactly as they are in a house circuit and operate from a pair of dry cells. Regulation house door bells and buttons are used. The batteries are mounted inside the box while the bells and buzzers are screwed on the inside so their tone is not muffled in any way by the walls of the box.

The sound of a telephone bell may be best obtained if the stage manager is fortunate enough to secure the real article from the local office of the telephone company, but barring this, the next best alternative is to use a door bell that in sound closely approaches that of a telephone bell. Telephone bells are placed in an inconspicuous place on the stage somewhere near the telephone so the distance between that instrument and the ringing of the bell does not seem incongruous.

Revolver Shots

Revolver shots offstage may be best obtained by using blank cartridges in a revolver or by striking a thick leather cushion a smart blow with a riding crop. The first is preferable although if the sound of the shot is supposed to occur at considerable distance, it may be necessary to fire the gun in one of the dressing rooms. Careful stage managers provide two guns for shots of any kind in the event that one revolver fails at the last moment. Incidentally, the firing of a revolver on the stage is always *covered* offstage by the stage manager. He has a gun cocked and ready to fire should the gun in the hands of the actor fail to go off at the right moment. This precaution may save an embarrassing moment.

Crashes

The crash effect most often called for in a play is that of either glass or chinaware. It is obtained by using a *crash box.* This is a box containing either broken glass or chinaware. At the proper moment, the contents of the box are dumped into another box on the floor with a resounding crash.

Banana or orange crates make excellent material for imitating the sound of crashing wood. The person who is responsible for the effect stands on a chair and jumps on the crate breaking it for the sound of splintering wood.

Explosions

All explosions do not sound alike. Distinct differences must be taken into account. The effect of a short, sharp explosion may be secured by firing a blank cartridge into an empty barrel, but most explosions carry with them the sound of falling debris. After the initial blast, one of the crash effects described above may be used or a *noise chute* may be constructed. This is made of boards and is about eight feet long. Slates are nailed across the bottom to add to the effect. To obtain the rumble of a heavy explosion, a basketful of small rocks is dumped down the chute. A roll on a kettle drum may also be used to gain the rumbling effect of an explosion.

Bricks

The appearance of a well constructed Colonial fireplace can be vastly improved in the following manner: Cut out pieces of composition board to the regulation size of bricks and coat them thinly with glue. Saw dust is then sprinkled over the glue to give the rough effect of bricks. After the glue has thoroughly dried, the bricks are painted with scene color and glued to the fireplace.

Stained Glass Windows

Stained glass windows for the stage are painted on window screen. The colors are applied by mixing small quantities of liquid dye with gelatine, the kind of clear gelatine that is used in making desserts. The colors dry on the screen in clear semi-transparent shades. The effect of leading in between the colored areas is obtained by painting with black enamel. A floodlight is used behind a stained glass window to get the full effect of the color. In dissolving the gelatine, keep it at a thicker consistency than the manufacturer recommends.

Engines

There is practically no limit to the ingenuity that can be exercised in the construction of offstage machinery effects. Toy ratchets and rattles play a most important part. The sound of a small steam engine such as is used in hoisting heavy beams or on a steam shovel is constructed as shown in Fig. 28. It is made of wood. The tin can on the long swinging arm may be one of those in which theatrical powder comes. It should have a screw top and is filled about one quarter full with small BB shot. As the handle is turned, the can swings back and forth. The moving shot gives a fine imitation of a steam engine. In cases of emergency, it is not necessary to build the entire apparatus. The can need only be shaken by hand with a steady, rhythmic motion.

The gear box of a hand turned emery wheel is very useful in making high speed mechanical effects. The emery wheel is removed and a wooden disc substituted as shown in Fig. 28 to make the effect of a riveting machine. Four short leather straps are spaced evenly about the wheel. They are just long enough to strike a glancing blow at a nearby metal plate. A short bolt is fastened in the end of each strap. By revolving the machine at high speed, the bolts strike the metal plate in rapid succession and give the sound of the riveting machine. The metal plate should not be fastened too rigidly to its supports. It should be allowed to vibrate freely.

Trains

Offstage train effects can be created with remarkable fidelity, but it requires considerable practice to co-ordinate the various elements into one unified effect of a train starting or stopping. The long distance puffing of a train is made by rubbing a wire coat hanger over three or four screen door springs. The springs are fastened into a shallow, flat box. (Fig. 28.) The ends of the box are made of one-inch lumber about three inches wide. The top and bottom are made of light veneer. It may be necessary to cut sound holes in these pieces to get the full effect. The box has no sides. The coat hanger is inserted through a side opening and rubbed back and forth in the rhythm of a puffing train.

The rumble of a heavy train approaching a station is obtained by wheeling a heavy hand truck over a sheet of corrugated iron placed on the floor. The hiss of escaping steam comes from a small tin whistle. The sound of the bell must, of course, come from a real bell approximating in size those used on a real locomotive.

Whistles

Large wooden whistles are sold which resemble in tone the whistle either of a train or a steamboat. They are rea-

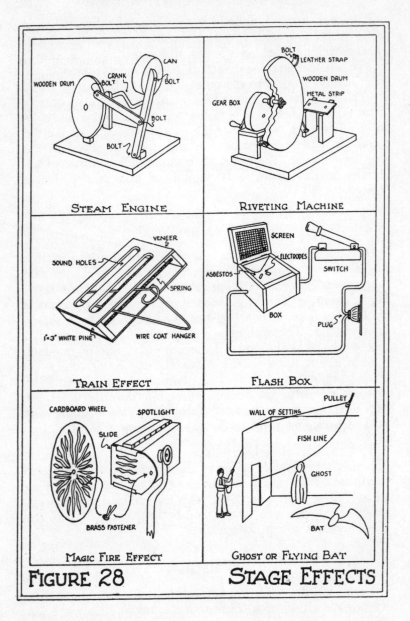

FIGURE 28   STAGE EFFECTS

sonable in price and are to be preferred over any home-made device, but the tone of a smaller wooden or tin whistle can be deepened by blowing it through a sounding box made of light veneer. The sounding box is a hollow square about four by four inches and eighteen inches to two feet long. The whistle is held in the mouth and the sounding box is inserted over it with one end held close to the face.

Magic Fire

Magical and supernatural plays often contain effects which at first glance seem almost impossible of achievement, but the modern magic of electricity is often more potent than anything commonly practiced by the ancients.

A puff of smoke and some magical character appears! The puff of smoke comes from a *flash box*. This is a small box containing two electrodes and a pinch or two of blasting or photographer's flashlight powder. A touch of the switch raises a column of smoke behind which the character appears. The flash box need not be over four inches square. The inside of the box is built into a little trough with the two electrodes projecting through the bottom about one-eighth inch apart. The trough is lined with a piece of asbestos to prevent the box from catching fire. The flash box should also be equipped with a little screen cover to allow the smoke to come through, and at the same time prevent the occurrences of stray sparks. (Fig. 28.)

"Magic fire" will increase the potency of the effect. It is made by using a spotlight containing a bright red or magenta medium. Over this is placed a cardboard slide containing several wavy slots. A cardboard wheel is fastened to one of the slides with a small bolt or brass paper fastener. The same wavy slots are cut around the entire surface of the wheel. By turning the wheel, and passing these slots in rapid succession over the slots in the slide, the effect of a quivering, dancing fire is achieved. (Fig. 28.)

Incidentally, by using a blue-green color medium, the same effect may be employed in creating the appearance of moonlight on waves. Behind a *scrim* of gauze curtain, it has been used successfully in creating the effect of an underwater scene.

Transparencies

Transparencies might also be classified under the heading of magical effects. Briefly, it is a scrim or gauze behind which characters mysteriously appear. It is used in the frame of pictures when living figures, supposedly inanimate, are to be seen through the frame. On occasion, a piece of gauze is inserted in the actual wall of a setting and painted on the surface to match the remaining wall space. By dimming the light on the stage and slowly increasing the intensity of the light behind the scrim, figures can be made to appear in a blank space on the wall. The effect is quite common in operettas or mystery plays and is used to convey the thoughts of individual characters or the actions of a dream.

Ghosts and Bats

The magical appearance of ghosts or bats in a mystery play is usually accomplished by threading these unearthly manifestations on a stout fish line (Fig. 28). The fishline is continuous and operates through an opening in the setting and a small pulley overhead. If the setting has a ceiling, the line runs through a small hole cut in the ceiling.

The ghosts and bats are constructed on wire frames. The bats are covered with black sateen while white cheese cloth has been known to make very effective ghosts. The appearance of ghostliness is enhanced by touching up the cheese cloth with patches of luminous paint.

Aeroplanes and Automobiles

The steady hum of an automobile or aeroplane engine is made by holding a small piece of cardboard against the revolving blades of an electric fan. A little practice will enable the operator to obtain the effect of starting and stopping or running at high speeds. There is no real substitute for imitating the sound of an automobile horn. It must be the real thing.

Projections

In these days of suggestive scenery, large images are frequently cast on a flat background by means of light. These scenic images may include everything from clouds and trees to huge buildings or the skeleton framework of large pieces of machinery. The effect is made by cutting the desired image in a square of cardboard and fitting it over a flood or spotlight. Allowance must always be made for

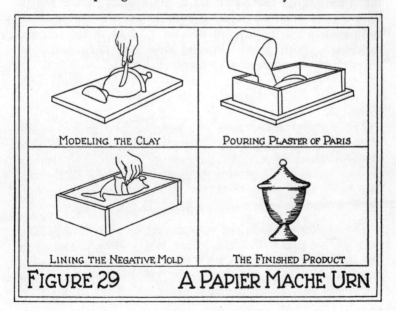

MODELING THE CLAY

POURING PLASTER OF PARIS

LINING THE NEGATIVE MOLD

THE FINISHED PRODUCT

FIGURE 29   A PAPIER MACHE URN

the angle at which the image strikes the flat surface. It is usually necessary to experiment and cut several cardboard slides before a satisfactory one is obtained.

Papier Mache

There are many small, irregular objects used on a stage such as architectural ornaments that can only be effectively made by casting them in papier mache. The process is not beyond the capabilities of the most modest craftsman. The first step is to model the desired object in clay. A framework is then built large enough to enclose a clay model on all sides. The model is coated with a covering of sweet oil applied with a brush, and afterwards, Plaster of Paris is poured to form the mould. The entire mold is then pried from the modeling board and the clay removed from the Plaster of Paris to form the *negative mold*. This is lined with glue soaked bits of newspaper to a depth of about one-sixteenth inch. It will be easier to remove the papier mache model if the negative mold also is coated with sweet oil before the lining process begins. After the paper is thoroughly dry and the glue hard, the finished product is gently pried from the Plaster of Paris mold and painted in the appropriate colors (Fig. 29).

Chapter V

CUTTING CORNERS ON COST

The rental of complete sets of costumes for productions such as *The Taming of the Shrew* or *The Merchant of Venice* is almost certain to be prohibitive for any but the larger high schools. The silks, satins, and brocades that seem to be needed for homemade costumes are likewise too expensive. It is not until the prospective producer examines some of the cheaper materials and realizes their potential beauty that the possibility of staging a costume play presents itself.

The theatrical uses of these cheaper materials have all been developed on the amateur stage, in Little Theatres and schools. They are suggested here because countless directors have used them before and found them ideally suited for their respective purposes.

The Fine Art of Substitution

Cheaper materials substituted for their richer counterparts should be chosen with an eye toward use. That is, the surface of the material is important. It should roughly resemble that of its more expensive sister. Then, too, the draping qualities should be similar. The stiff folds of satin are best imitated in the cheaper sateens. Canton flannel likewise makes an excellent substitute for felt or velvet.

Cheese cloth, voile, and old lace curtains can be used to suggest fine linen, veiling, chiffons, and laces. Flowered silkoline of the type sold for comforters is splendid for dance costumes and period plays. Calico, challie, cotton crepe, cheesecloth, broadcloth, cotton prints, and organdy all have their uses. Certain kinds of damask will serve as brocade. Oil cloth can be used for boots and shoes. Unbleached muslin, because it can be dyed, will serve in multitudes of ways.

In any event, it will pay the prospective costume director

to search the shelves and remnant counters of the local stores. Investigate, too, the drapery goods counter. Quite often drapery remnants of exquisite material can be purchased at a bargain price. Nothing quite equals the thrill of discovering for the stage a cheap material that under the lights appears to be one of the most expensive fabrics obtainable.

Also, many schools will be able to obtain their cloth from a wholesale house. Where large numbers of identical costumes are to be made, as for a musical chorus, this is the ideal way to purchase the material.

Theatrical Fabrics

Of the strictly theatrical fabrics sold by companies engaging in this business, there are a handful which the amateur producer will find invaluable.

First among these fabrics is cotton-backed duvetyne. It resembles suede cloth in appearance. It is moderately priced and comes in some forty-one myriad shades. Innumerable uses can be found for duvetyne. In fact, the authors had occasion to use it for a complete set of male costumes in *The Taming of the Shrew,* for breeches, doublets, capes, and surcoats. It suggests royal velvet; in proper shades it imitates suede or soft buckskin; it can be used for wool. Its uses are almost limitless. It is easy to sew; it does not fray easily, and thus, the seams need not be sewed quite so securely as with other fabrics of a similar weave. Whatever the play or whatever the period, it will pay the costumer to become thoroughly acquainted with all the qualities of this amazing cloth.

Other theatrical fabrics are the cotton-backed satins and velveteens which have all the appearance of their more expensive counterparts. China silk, of a very light weight and gauzy texture, can be bought quite cheaply. Georgettes and chiffons can be obtained at half of their usual cost. Celanese taffeta and brilliant faille, in a host of colors, and panne lustre and faille satin in rayon mixture, though difficult to sew, do offer a wide variety of colors and weaves.

In addition, the gold, silver, and bronze metallic clothes are best obtained from theatrical companies.

Buckram, tarlatane, and crinoline are very important for re-inforcing collars and cuffs and for making ruffs. Tarlatane is especially excellent for this latter purpose as it need not be hemmed. It is available in thirty or more hues suitable for every purpose imaginable.

Spangles, ribbons, and gold braid for dance costumes and for decoration should be bought from the theatrical supply houses as they usually have lower prices and more of a stock than local dealers.

Companies specializing in this type of material are all listed in the bibliography and most of them will be glad to mail a complete range of prices and samples upon request.

Consistency

The important thing to remember when substituting cheaper materials is that they must be used consistently. An entire set of classic costumes can be made of cheese-cloth with startling effect, but the use of one silk costume will mar the whole ensemble. If Shakespearean costumes are made of dyed unbleached muslin, then use no velvet, or the one velvet costume will intrude like the proverbial sore thumb and completely ruin the effect of the others. Duve-tyne is the one exception to this rule for it looks equally well with any material and especially rich with silk. The material to be used for costuming is really unimportant so long as this one rule of consistency throughout the whole ensemble is closely observed.

Accessories

There are as-many substitutes for the genuine in trim-mings and accessories as there are in the use of materials. It is well to remember that jewelry, trimmings, and the like are all seen from a distance. They must be visible. It will not pay a member of the costume committee to sew tiny white beads on the front panel of Bianca's dress when, from the audience, they will not be seen five feet from the stage.

The variety and ten cent stores are excellent places to go shopping for jewelry. Jeweled reflector buttons, used by many car owners in fastening on their license plates, make excellent rubies or emeralds. And one must stop at the jewelry section for "rings, and things, and fine array."

Second hand stores, white elephant shops, and rummage sales should all be investigated for what they may offer in the way of jewelry and accessories. Then, too, one should not neglect sending out a call to private homes where frequently old strings of beads, bracelets, brooches, and the like go begging for want of use and are packed away in the family attic. And hardware stores should not be forgotten. Chains bought from the latter and nicely gilded will serve very well.

Excellent brooches may be made by sewing bright beads on a stiff-backed piece of buckram or cardboard. Large pendants can be fashioned by gluing the reflector light from the mud guard of a bicycle on a properly cut piece of painted plywood.

Gold and silver chains result from gilding or painting safety chains, furnace chains, safety pins from shower curtains hooked together, washers, or a section of dog leash.

The roofing caps used to fasten down tar paper have a variety of uses in forming large ear-rings, or bangles, or bracelets.

In making chain armor, mop cloth, obtained from the janitor supply companies and dyed gray, is the most successful substitute. Helmets and plate armor can be fashioned of oilcloth or the metal cloths. Papier mache is also useful in reproducing the latter, but more about this later in the section devoted to the costumes of the Middle Ages.

Nor, in this matter of accessories, will the costume director omit the commercial costume companies. Their sample kits contain a multitude of trimmings, spangles, laces, and braids, all of which are modestly priced.

Tights

Shakespearean plays, for the most part, require tights for the costumes of the male characters, and these offer a problem in themselves for the director who must watch costs.

It is always best to use the regular article whenever possible. Get white ones from a theatrical or athletic goods dealer and dye them to the required shades. Be careful to allow for shrinkage when purchasing.

It is, however, possible to use makeshift tights if the trunks of the costumes are not too short. Opera hose can be purchased in a variety of colors and used by sewing them to trunks or dancing tights. They may be obtained in silk or lisle.

Perhaps, the cheapest method of simulating tights, is through the use of hockey hose which may be obtained from athletic goods dealers. Unfortunately, though, these come only in black and thus are not as adaptable, but they do cut the cost of tights in half. They can be used for many purposes, however. The writers used them with every costume in *The Taming of the Shrew* without spoiling the color scheme at all.

Boots and Shoes

Boots and shoes frequently play a major part in giving a costume its appearance of reality. Here again, ingenuity on the part of costumer will save many pennies for the finance committee.

Medieval shoes may be nothing more than heavy wool stockings, cut or laced up the leg or rolled down to the ankle. An inner sole of cardboard placed in the bottom of the stocking gives the foot more protection.

Sandals may be suggested by using inner soles, the kind most frequently used for bedroom slippers, with lacings fastened across them. The dancing sandals in natural suede serve very well, too.

Elizabethan shoes for men may be suggested by fashioning pieces of black oil cloth like a low spat so that they cover the lacings of a modern oxford. Rosettes may be added for decoration. They are anchored with elastic straps of black going under the instep. Dark leather bedroom slippers, or better, the Congress house shoe or Romeo slipper serves very well.

Boot tops can be made of duvetyne re-inforced with buckram as shown in the frontispiece. Oil cloth may be used also. Jockey or Russian boots may be nothing more difficult than black oil cloth for the leg section anchored below the instep with elastic bands.

In this entire matter of accessories or substitution of materials, one must remember that it is frequently the suggestion which gives the effect. A good imitation, viewed from the audience, oftimes gives a better impression than the genuine article. The fact that the cost of production was cut in half makes no difference to the audience if the effect is good. They will never see the balance sheet.

Chapter VI

THE ELEMENTS OF COLOR

The members of an audience may leave an amateur play feeling vaguely dissatisfied and yet not know why. The acting was good; the play moved along rapidly; yet, there was something that marred the effect. It was the *visual* memory of the production that failed to please.

Two girls, one in a red-violet dress, the other in red, often stood side by side; the mother in her blue-violet robe sat on a blue-green divan; the hero, in his suit of blue-green, wore a flaming red tie. Was it these combinations of colors that spoiled the whole effect of the play? Most assuredly, it was, for whether or not the audience could name a reason for that vague feeling of dissatisfaction, those colors produced a bad response.

It is when we understand fully the use and the meaning of color that the best effect is obtained in the costumes of a play.

The Color System

For convenience, colors are most often grouped together under the Prang System. There are other systems of color, but the Prang System is most easily understood by the beginner and will be used here.

There are three *Primary Colors* in the Prang System. These are Red, Blue, and Yellow. They cannot be obtained by mixing other colors, therefore the name. Together, they form what is known as the Primary Triad or *harmony*, that is, these three colors may be used together without "clashing."

When two Primary Colors are mixed a *Secondary Color* is formed: Red and Blue to make Violet, Yellow and Blue to make Green, and Yellow and Red to make Orange.

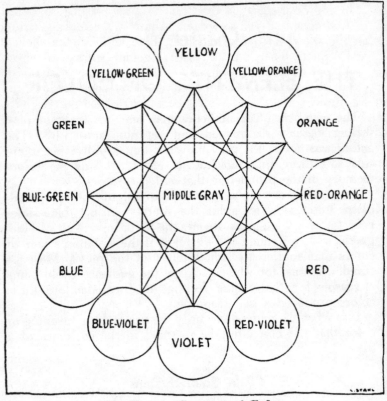

The Prang System of Color

Likewise, these three colors may be used together in what is called a Secondary Triad or harmony.

Hue Triads are formed when a Primary is mixed with a Secondary: Yellow with Orange to form Yellow-Orange, Blue with Green to form Blue-Green, and so on. The two basic Hue Triads are Yellow-Green, Red-Orange, Blue-Violet; and Yellow-Orange, Red-Violet, and Blue-Green.

Ideally, triad harmonies are used with only one color in its full intensity. The other two colors are *neutralized*, *i.e.*, mixed with the opposing color (their complement) on the color wheel to give them a "grayed" effect.

In addition, colors in the Prang System may be combined in *Complementary Harmonies*. There are opposing colors on the wheel as Green and Red, Blue and Orange, Yellow and Violet. They may be used together with good effect.

A *Split Complement* is achieved by using the *three* colors opposite any single color on the wheel: as Yellow and the three violets, Red-Violet, Blue-Violet, and pure Violet.

As with the triads, more subtle and artistic effects are obtained by neutralizing one color of the complementary harmonies with its opposite to give a grayed effect. As with a split complement, each of the violets, or only one or two, may be mixed with a bit of yellow to reduce their intensity.

Analogous Harmonies are those which are "near" to each other, Yellow-Orange, Yellow, and Yellow-Green. Such *similar* colors may be used together without fear of clashing.

To summarize at this point, we learn that the following facts are true about the color wheel in its relation to costume:

1. Any half of the color wheel will give contrast. For instance, any or all of the colors may be used from Yellow down to Violet in devising a costume plot. There will be harmony and sufficient contrast *providing* some colors are used in their neutral shades.

2. Any quarter of the color wheel may be used to achieve harmony. This is similar to an analogous harmony. There will be harmony without the contrast evident by using a full half of the wheel.

3. Two or three adjacent (analogous) colors can be neutralized (grayed) by using the complement of the middle color.

4. Adjacent colors may be used together in any quantity.

5. Bright colors (the Primaries and the Secondaries) should be relieved by white and black or neutral colors.

6. Bright colors may all be linked with one dominant color to avoid disturbing contrast or clash in what is known as a "Japanese" harmony.

Colors have other qualities not discoverable on the wheel of the Prang System, that is, *intensity* and *value*.

The intensity of a color is its nearness to gray. As was said before, when a color is mixed with its complement, as Red with Green, a grayed or more sombre Red is produced. Likewise with Green: A duller Green is produced when mixed with Red.

Colors neutralized in this manner are not apt to have the glaring effect so often the case when used in their full intensity. With neutralized or grayed colors, it is easier to achieve harmony between the costumes than is the case if pure color is used.

Value is the nearness of a color to Black or White. Red mixed with White produces Pink. Pink is a "high" value of Red. It reflects a greater quantity of light than will pure Red. Conversely, Green mixed with Black will be "low" in value. It reflects less light and will be more subdued and recessive in tone.

From this, we discover two more summarizing facts about the use of color in relation to costume:

1.   Very light values (pastel shades) may always be used together with good effect.

2.   Very dull intensities (grays) of any and all colors are good.

Commercial colors, known variously under such intriguing names as *dubonnet, heather,* and *wheat,* are merely graduations in intensity and value of the old familiar colors around the wheel. The names mean little and are new each year. By comparing these colors with basic tones about the wheel, it is quite possible to achieve harmonies based on the above systems with any fabric however different.

Colors also have the quality of being either "warm" or "cool". Yellow and Reds, or colors which may be obtained by mixing these two, are definitely warm colors. Colors with large component parts of Blue, or Blue itself, are cool. These two facts will be examined more closely when the psychological aspects of color are discussed, but for the present, the following two additions are true:

1. Dark complexioned individuals appear best in warm colors.

2. Blonde persons should wear cool colors unless the personality is strong enough to counteract the effect of a warm color.

The Effect of Light on Color

The costumer will soon discover that stage lights have the habit of doing peculiar things to color. The costume which was supposed to be a bright, spirited red fades to a pale, sickly orange beneath amber light. Dark blue retreats into a muddy green. This fact, unless foreseen, can lead to much wailing and gnashing of teeth. There is no one quite so unhappy as the costume director whose best effects are ruined on the night of the production by lighting which totally changes the color scheme.

There are a number of tables and light charts purporting to show the effect of light on color, but at best, such tables are only approximate. It is better by far to test each piece of material under the lights to be used in the performance before going ahead with the costumes. There is no guesswork then; the final effect can be seen and judged. Texture and weave often have as much to do with the appearance of fabric under light as color alone.

Making a Light Box: Should it prove impossible to test fabrics under the actual conditions of stage lighting, the use of a *light box* is recommended. This is nothing more nor less than a wooden box about two feet square with a light-tight door on one end. It is painted dead black inside. Three bulbs (one Red, one Blue, one Amber) similar to those used on the stage circuits are wired on the end of the box opposite the door. To operate, the colors to be used on any specific costume or group of costumes are hung over a rack or thumbtacked to the door end of the box. By turning on any combination of lights on the other end of the

box and peering through a couple of eye-holes, very much
in the manner of an old parlor sterioptican, a good idea
of the effect of colored light on any fabric can be obtained.

The Psychology of Color

Almost more important than the scientific facts about
color are its psychological aspects. Colors, through long
use, association, or poetic conception, have come to mean
various things. Certain colors are proper to certain persons or things or express certain moods. When we "see
red" we think of anger and heat. We are accustomed to
thinking of white in connection with purity. Light colors
suggest ethereal things; more sombre hues bespeak of
tragedy and sorrow.

The costumer cannot afford to neglect these attributes
of color in designing costumes for the stage. The dramatic
values of the script can be heightened or subdued by the
dress of the characters. In fact, as in certain types of
dramas, pageants, dance dramas, and the like, the entire
dramatic impact can be made or destroyed by the effective
use of costume.

To better understand this use of color, they are presented
here with some of their common psychological associations:

I. Red.
   A. The color of blood.
      It suggests anger, passion, murder, destruction,
      shame, stimulation, tragedy, and hatred.
   B. The color of fire.
      Suggesting warmth, power, vigor, energy, cour-
      age, and haste.
   C. Through long association, red is also the color of
      royalty and Cardinals.

II. Orange.
   A. In nature, the color of autumn and harvest. In
      this connection, it suggests contentment, warmth,
      plenty, and cheerful laughter.

    B.   It is mildly the color of fire and flames, suggesting here passion and mild unrest.

III. Yellow (Bright).

    A.   In nature, the color of sunlight and harvest, the bright summertime.
        Suggests gaiety, joy, wisdom, and love.

    B.   As the color of gold it suggests gaudiness and power.

IV. Yellow (Dingy).

    A.   Suggestive of jealousy, inconstancy, deceit, decay, indecency, and sickness.

    B.   As the symbol of cowardice, this color suggests faithlessness and treason.

V. Green.

    A.   In nature, green is chiefly the color of springtime suggesting life, hope, inspiration, vitality, youth, vigor, immaturity, and victory. It is also the color of the woods and the sea, in this connection, suggesting solitude, peace, and eternity.

    B.   It is also the color of mystery, magicians, and weird, slimy things. It stands for jealousy, i.e., the "green-eyed" monster.

VI. Blue.

    A.   Blue is the color of the heavens, the sky, the water. In this connection, it suggests truth, quietness, peace, stability, hope, spirituality, and fidelity in love. As the color of night, it suggests romance and love.

    B.   In life, blue is associated with a state of depression known as the "blues"

VII. Violet (Purple).

    A.   Suggests royalty, majesty, great wealth and riches, and heroic virtue.

    B. Old age—suffering, seriousness, passion, temperance, and martyred truth.

VIII. Black—The lack of all color.

    A. Suggests death and the absence of things, woe, horror, despair, depression, torture, and mourning.

    B. Witchcraft and magic—Mystery, evil, crime, and shame.

    C. In a religious connection, black suggests the habit of monks and nuns and deep penitence.

IX. White—The presence of all colors.

    A. In nature, white indicates the winter with snow and frost. It suggests purity, innocence, holiness, faith, delicacy, and chastity.

    B. In life, it suggests deity, angels, saints, or virgins, integrity, humility, modesty, femininity, and truth.

X. Black and White.

    A. The presence of all things (white) and the absence of all things (black) suggests sophistication, extreme contrast.

From all the foregoing, it can be readily seen that color must play a very important part in any scheme of production. Color in costume broadcasts to the audience the type of character who wears the costume and his relation to the rest of the cast. It can be the key by which the audience opens doors to new enjoyment of the play.

Color in Costume

The most important characters always dominate the color scheme. Hamlet wears black, but against the colorful costumes of the Danish court, Hamlet is distinct; he stands apart. If a leading woman character must wear pastel shades to suggest her role, then no other costume must appear to overshadow hers. In *Daddy Longlegs*, for instance, the ingenue, Judy, because of the nature of her part, must wear light colors. A brilliant red dress on one of the minor characters would completely destroy the leading character's dominance whenever it appeared.

With white or light costumes worn by the leading characters, the remainder of the cast must wear rich, dark clothing as a means of contrast.

Characters in a play who are mutually harmonious should suggest their relationship by being garbed in neighboring hues. Adversely, conflict and struggle between opposing parties can be indicated through the use of complementary or opposing harmonies. As in *Romeo and Juliet*, for instance, Romeo's family, the Montagues, might well be dressed in tones of red. The Capulets, to show the distinction, might wear various tones of green. The opposition would be established. In their costumes, Romeo and Juliet might well betray their relationship by wearing subtle bits of green and red respectively. The mob and various minor characters appearing throughout the play can indicate their status by wearing neutralized shades of either color.

To show how color planning along these methods works, herewith is presented the color chart of costumes for *The Taming of the Shrew* as presented by the authors. The costumes are Italian of the Elizabethan Period, about 1600. The important characters are alone included:

Costume Plot for *The Taming of the Shrew*.

Petruchio—The most important male character, a fiery, vigorous individual.

1. Use tones of red; brown and buffs intensified with crimson. The latter (red-red-orange) will also link him with Katherine.

2. Blue-green in feather of hat for contrast.

Katherine—The female lead, passionate, shrewish, spirited.

1. Vigorous intensities of red or red-red-orange modified by trimmings of cream plus a bit of blue-green for

contrast. A red-red-orange dress with a cream front panel, cream-colored lace. Introduce a bit of blue-green-blue in the design at the bottom of the skirt panel and possibly a touch of jewelry.

2. In her wedding gown of white, Katherine effects her change of character and thus the last scene of the play is enhanced when she appears still in white suggesting faithfulness, modesty, and feminine truth.

Lucentio—The juvenile romantic lead who wins Bianca.

Suggest youth and victory as well as the color of spring by using a shade of green. Since Lucentio is not involved in a struggle, do not use a contrasting color for trimming but rather an analogous warm color, a tone of yellow indicating constancy and love.

Bianca—The obedient young sister, feminine and lovely.

To link her with Lucentio as well as to suggest her youth and mildness, use tints of green in light intensity. Jade, perhaps, is the best popular name. Cream, a tint of yellow, offers the correct trim and relates her to her sister.

Hortensio—A friend of Petruchio, the rejected suitor of Bianca, he is mild and proud in his bearing.

Shades of violet, deep purple for the doublet with mauve for the tights. Since this color suggests wealth, it will also serve to link him with the widow.

Widow—A minor character spoken of as wealthy and kind.

Use tints of violet slightly greyed with cream trimming and a touch of blue for contrast.

Baptista—The father, "an affable and courteous gentleman."

Black is best for him since he must be linked with several colorful characters. Gold, suggesting his power and wealth, is adequate for trimming, a gold chain, a gilded staff, etc.

Gremio—A wealthy old rake.

Gold (yellow), which suggests his gaudiness, offset with black for his age will best define him.

Vincentio—The aged father of Lucentio.

He should appear in black with white for contrast. He is a minor character and must not be too emphatic.

The important servants should echo their masters in milder hues coupled with neutrals.

Tranio—Lucentio's man.

He may well appear in tan, a shade of gold, with green as trimming.

Grumio—Petruchio's faithful servant.

Buff with rose trim.

Biondello—Lucentio's servant.

Brown with soiled green tights.

From the foregoing, one can readily see that color has an important part in weaving and intensifying the story of a play. It is color, handled like this and worked out in detail before the work of actually making the costumes begins, that adds so much to the spectator's appreciation of drama as a work of art.

COSTUME SKETCH

Petruchio in THE TAMING OF THE SHREW

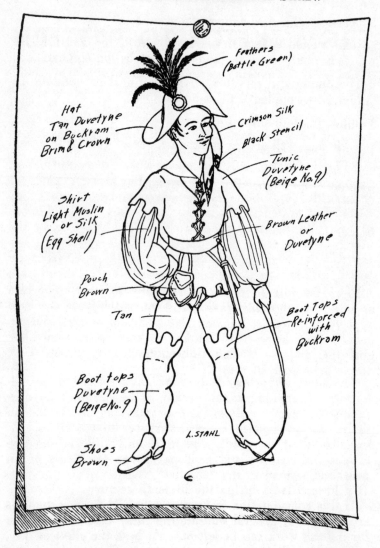

Feathers
(Battle Green)

Hat
Tan Duvetyne
on Buckram
Brim & Crown

Crimson Silk

Black Stencil

Tunic
Duvetyne
(Beige No.9)

Shirt
Light Muslin
or Silk
(Egg Shell)

Brown Leather
or
Duvetyne

Pouch
Brown

Tan

Boot Tops
Re-inforced
with
Buckram

Boot tops
Duvetyne
(Beige No.9)

L. STAHL

Shoes
Brown

Chapter VII

FROM SKETCH TO PATTERN

The work of making costumes begins with the sketch. This may be either an art class project or the work of students outside of school. Artistically, it may be anything desired, but the finished sketch would include every detail of form and decoration which the designer wishes to have appear in the finished costume.

Colored sketches may be made with either transparent colors or tempera, the latter being the cheaper kinds of show-card colors obtainable at any art store. Sketches may be finished in pencil or pen. In these cases, small swatches of the material to be used are clipped along side of the sketch to show the makers the texture and color to be followed in the finished costume. Of course, if a color harmony for the production is decided upon before the sketches are made, it is only necessary to show which colors are used in little marginal notes—as was done on the frontispiece of this book.

The Silhouette

The most important feature of any costume is its silhouette. Every important period in history had its own peculiar costume outline. The proportions of the human figure, as revealed in clothes, varied with the times. To visualize what is meant, one need only look at the two dresses outlined on the next page, one the dress of an American woman in the "eighties" and the other the dress of a French lady during the fifteenth century.

If this consideration is kept in mind, if each costume is accurate as to general outline, the fussy details that make for difficult work can be left out. At best, the effect of tiny, elaborate work is lost upon the stage. The striving is for

Two Silhouettes

the "big" effect in color and pattern. If the general silhouette of each period is faithfully followed, the audience will not mind or even notice the lack of minor detail.

About Costume Design

In designing a costume of any type, care should be taken to see that it fits the personality and temperament of the character who is to wear it. This was discussed somewhat under the psychology of color, but the cut and pattern will vary, too. As in *The Taming of the Shrew,* the costume of Petruchio, the wild young wooer, is distinctly different from that of Lucentio, the more earnest lover. His costume is rough and flamboyant, that of the latter's more refined and subdued. Likewise, the costumes of their servants vary. The costume of Gremio, the old suitor for Bianca's hand, is exaggerated in cut to betray his dandified character as an old roue.

Also, costumes should show their wearer's personal tastes and position in life. The clothes of the servant immediately stamp him as such.

Before beginning the costume designs, be sure to read the script of the play. Decide with the director what are to be the principal characteristics of each and every person in the play. Then, when this is in hand, go ahead with the designs seeking always to make these variations in character and personality apparent to the eyes of the audience at an instant's glance. At best, a play is a fleeting thing. It is when every element of the production, the acting, the lights, *and* the costumes, all blend together to form a unified picture that the audience carries away from the theatre a pleased and lasting impression of what they have seen.

To accomplish such an end, it is evident that the designer must have at hand some source material from which to work. This is not, however, as difficult as it sounds. It is usually unnecessary to plow through reams of books. A few well selected pictures of the period will give the designer a point of departure. From these, inspiration will do the rest. Minor details can be varied, changes made in the cut or pattern, decorations added or taken away. After all, costume making, like all work in the theatre, is pure creation. It is very unwise, not to say tragic, to force costume makers to avoid entirely the free way of the imagination.

Making the Patterns

The interpretation of a sketch, first, into a pattern, then, into the finished costume, appears at first blush to be a difficult business. It does require a certain knack. Once, however, that the costumer masters that knack, or happens to be born with it, there is no trouble at all in translating the most exotic sketch into the finished costume.

Professional costumers use a number of standard patterns cut to the average figure. They are based on the proportions of the average man with a 38" chest and the average woman with a 36" bust. Since, however, there is scarcely such a creature as a standard or average-size high school student, another method must be evolved for making patterns in school.

The pattern makers will do just as well to cut their patterns out of either wrapping paper or old newspapers. The cutting and fitting can be done by pinning the paper directly onto the person who is to wear the costume. General shapes of the various patterns are shown in the costume plates of this book. With the shape in mind, and the size and general conformation of the wearer directly before her, the cutter can then go ahead and snip and snap until the result is achieved.

In many cases, several completed portions of the pattern can be pinned together on the clothing of the person who is being fitted. Checking can be done in this way and a good idea obtained as to the final fit of the cloth.

Also, old clothes belonging to the wearer can be ripped apart and the resulting pieces used to provide patterns of very great accuracy. The latter method serves exceptionally well with shirts and coats.

To aid the business of getting a fit, a few general measurements should be taken from individual actors. The resulting figures can be used in checking the costume when the basting is done. For women, these may include:

A. The length of the skirt.

B. The measurement of the waist.

C. The measurement of the bust.

D. The neck measurement.

E. The measurement of the inner sleeve.

F. The measurement of the outside sleeve with the arm bent at the elbow.

For men, these include in addition to (A and B) the measurements of the waist and chest.

C. The measurement of the trousers or breeches down the outside seam.

D. The inseam measurement.

E. The neck measurement.

F. and G.—The inner and outer measurements of the sleeve.

On tight-fitting garments, it is also advisable to take measurements of the chest and back from shoulder to shoulder.

Measurements and the method of making them are shown on the drawing below. A sheet of paper containing this information should be clipped together with the costume sketch and the name of the actor for ready reference in the costume shop.

Making Measurements

Fitting and Sewing

Two fittings are generally essential for good costume work. One fitting is made when the costume is basted and the other for a final check-up when the costume is completed. First fittings may be made with the basted costume inside-out unless the actor is unusually lop-sided and the right sleeve must appear on that arm. Pins may be used to take up the seams where a snugger fit is desired, and a piece of colored chalk or a thin sliver of soap will serve to indicate where the costume is to be made larger.

Fit is the most important part of any stage costume. Care should be taken. Materials may be cheap; the sewing may not be of the best, but a sagging pair of breeches is instantly apparent.

For the final sewing, it is well to remember that the fine variety of stitching so desirable in clothing for the street is a total loss upon the stage. Serviceability is the main consideration. Heavy thread will not show. Simple stitching, briskly done, will speed up the work in the shop and will in no way destroy the appearance of the costume. In every case, too, allowance must be made for the actor's movements upon the stage. It will not do to make the armholes tight if the actor is to appear in a fencing scene.

The Costume Shop

Where only a few costumes are to be made, there is no great need for organization in the costume shop. But where a lot of them must be made in a short time, speed is essential.

Provide sufficient tools, pins and needles for everyone. A number of good sharp scissors in varying sizes should be available. If the school boasts only a single sewing machine, it may be possible to borrow one or more from the homes of the workers, or they can be rented very reasonably from the sewing machine companies. There should be a large work table of convenient height for laying out material while it is being cut; there should be safety pins and tape measures for everyone. Since most stage costumes are fastened with snaps or hooks and eyes, preferably the latter, these should be provided in quantity. In addition, there should be hangers and a rack on which to place the finished costumes. Nothing more quickly destroys the morale of the shop than to have a vital piece of some important costume disappear at the last moment after it has been "stored" by piling it away in a corner.

For best results, a special room should be assigned for the costume work. It can, then, be locked each night when the crew is through. Such a system obviates the necessity of packing up the work each night and minimizes the chance of items being lost. As in everything else, organization will pay in the costume shop.

Chapter VIII

COSTUME DESIGNS

The following pages detail a number of costumes of specific periods and types. In a volume of this kind, the listing can in nowise be complete, but found here will be costumes suitable for nearly every production attempted by the average high school.

Biblical Costumes

Costumes of this type will be found useful in plays and pageants both at Christmas and at Easter time. Variations in the cut and color of the clothing may be supplied by a study of pictures in Sunday School lesson leaflets or some such illustrated work as Hurlbut's *Story of the Bible*.

The basis of all Hebrew costume was the long tunic of linen reaching to the ankles. It was worn by both men and women alike. Men wore it with sleeves extending almost to the elbow while women most frequently wore long flowing sleeves down to the wrist. For the purposes of the stage, the garment can be made of unbleached muslin. It is fastened at the waist with a sash of colored material.

Over the tunic, was most frequently worn a mantle, affected by both men and women. Mantles were large squares of cloth draped over the left shoulder and about the body with the right hand free. The portion draped across the back could be raised to cover the head where it was often held in place by a colored band.

Turbans were also worn. Fashion a turban by taking a piece of material one yard wide and three or four yards long and wrap it round and round the head until the desired shape is obtained. Oftentimes, too, head coverings may be fashioned by taking a square yard of cloth and placing it over the head with the excess in back. Coverings

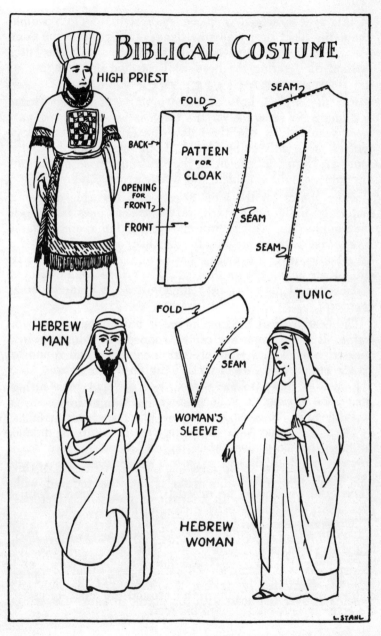

BIBLICAL COSTUME

HIGH PRIEST

FOLD

BACK

OPENING FOR FRONT

FRONT

PATTERN FOR CLOAK

SEAM

SEAM

SEAM

TUNIC

HEBREW MAN

FOLD

SEAM

WOMAN'S SLEEVE

HEBREW WOMAN

L. STAHL

of this type are held in place by a strip of cloth wound about the head or by narrow bands, two or three in number, made of light rope and covered with cloth. The latter method of covering the head is illustrated in the figure of the Hebrew woman.

For the high priests of the temple, a somewhat richer costume is in order. Over the tunic is worn a second garment reaching to slightly below the knees. It is heavily fringed and richly embroidered. If the sleeves of this outer tunic are short, as shown in the drawing, those of the under tunic should extend to the wrist in wide, full folds.

Outer tunics for the high priests may be made of richer materials, but for the stage, very excellent ones have been cut from burlap. The decoration, in imitation of embroidery, is applied with a brush. To do this, obtain dye in the little bottles used for making batiks and apply with a fairly stiff brush in the design desired. The fringe on the sleeves and bottom of the tunic are remnants from a drapery goods counter.

The headdress of the high priest is built upon a buckram frame. It is hollow in the center, shaped like a high crown, and strips of cloth are merely wrapped round and round to give it body. Two feet of cloth hang down the back.

Both men and women may wear a sort of loose-fitting cloak over the tunic. Such a cloak has voluminous sleeves reaching to the bottom of the garment. They hang in folds. Cloaks can be cut from two widths of the material folded as shown in the drawing.

It is unnecessary to do any hemming on costumes of this type. The borders of the material may be relieved with dyed designs applied with a brush or gold and silver ribbon may be sewed in place on the richer garments.

Sandals are worn on the feet. For the stage, these may be either acrobatic dancing sandals or straw slippers imported from the Orient. These latter are very cheap and may be recommended if an additional strap or band of cloth is provided at the heel and around the ankle to assist the actor in keeping them on his feet.

Costumes of this character are worn in Nativity plays and Passion plays and pageants. Familiar dramatic characters of the period are Mary and Joseph, the Shepherds, the Hebrew kings of the nativity plays, the Three Wise Men, the Twelve Apostles, Jesus, and Esther.

Paintings which may be used as an indication of color and costume are: The Sistine Madonna by Raphael, Christ Before the Doctors by Hoffman, The Last Supper by Leonardo da Vinci, and The Adoration of the Magi by Botticelli.

The Greeks and Romans

The costumes of the Greeks and Romans are not as common as they used to be in our stage productions, but they do have their uses. Spring dance festivals and May Fetes often use this type of costume. Symbolical figures of Truth, Justice, and Purity all wear costumes of the Greek and Roman classic period.

The Greeks: The tunic or *chiton*, as it is called, is basis of all Greek costume. For stage use, it may be made of soft cheesecloth or *crepe de Chine*. It is never pressed. In fact, the appearance of the costume will be much improved if it is thoroughly wetted before wearing and allowed to dry in a long, tight roll. The resulting wrinkles allow the costume to hang in soft, tiny folds emulating closely the effect of draperies seen on the statues of ancient Greece.

Tunics for men are made in one piece. They encircle the body on the right side under the arm and fasten over the left shoulder with a small clasp or pin. They reach to the knees or a trifle below and are held in at the waist with a sash or cord.

Women's tunics are longer, ankle length or nearly so, and are made to fasten at both shoulders with ornamental clasps. The simple tunic or chiton was further fastened by a long cord passed around the waist, over the shoulders, then down the back and around the waist as shown in the drawing.

With both men and women, a *super-tunic* was often worn. The super-tunic was merely an additional length at the top

GREEK AND ROMAN COSTUME

GREEK MAN

GREEK WOMAN

SIMPLE TUNIC

TUNIC OR CHITON
WITH FOLDED SUPER-TUNIC

FOLDED TOGA

ROMAN WOMAN

ROMAN MAN

L. STAHL

of the chiton folded over and allowed to drape down to the waist.

All-over designs of simple figures or plain borders in gold, silver, or colors may be used tó relieve the plain cloth of chitons. Colors can best be applied with batik dyes and a brush. With gold and silver, the dry, powdered paint is used, the kind applied to radiators. The powder is mixed with a *bronzing liquid* supplied for the purpose and applied with a brush. For all such work, it is best to thumbtack the material to a wooden frame while the painting is being done.

In addition, the Greeks wore the *peplos,* a large, oblong piece of material about two yards wide and four yards long. This was wound twice around the body under the arms before passing it up over the shoulders. It was so worn that the back portions of it could be pulled up over the head for extra protection.

The Romans: Roman costumes may be made of light, unbleached muslin left in its natural, somewhat tawny color.

A tunic was worn. For men, it reached to the knees while women wore theirs ankle length. It may be fashioned similar to the tunic worn by the Jews described in the previous section, though with women, the upper part of the sleeve was often left open and fastened with clasps, an elaboration of the method of fastening the Greek chiton. Tunics were fastened at the waist with a cloth band by men and by cords wound about the figure by women in a manner very similar to that of the Greeks. Long extra lengths of the cord hung down to the hem of the garment in front after being knotted at the waist.

The *toga* is the distinctive garment of Roman men. Though made in one piece, it is formed of two distinctive parts: A full semi-circle with a diameter three times that of the wearer and a smaller segment of a circle of the same length. The latter, narrower portion of the toga is folded over the former and the whole draped about the figure with the smaller piece on the outside.

To drape a toga properly, drop one corner of the folded semi-circle over the left shoulder until it reaches the ankle in front. Then, pass the remaining folds of the material behind the back and under the right arm. Throw the remaining end of the semi-circle over the left shoulder. If the toga has been correctly cut, the second end should hang to the ankles in back. It is draped rather loosely in front to form graceful folds.

Roman women of good standing never wore the toga. In its place, a long, oblong cloth with decorative borders was draped about the figure in a manner similar to that employed by the Greeks in wearing the peplos.

Both Greek and Roman costumes will hang much better if they are adequately weighted at the corners with lead dress weights. For instance, a weight may be sewed in each end corner of the toga. On mantles, a weight should be sewed in each corner to assist the draping process.

Jewelry was worn, especially by the women. Rings for the fingers and ears are both in order. In addition, women may wear a kind of tiara-like headdress fashioned of jewels (beads sewed onto cloth, buckram, or threaded onto a light wire frame).

Sandals covered the feet. For women, since their dresses are rather long, ballet slippers or acrobatic dancing sandals may be worn. For men, it may be well to investigate the possibilities of the soft leather insoles obtainable at the ten cent store. Narrow straps of cloth or leather may be sewed to these and the whole fastened onto the foot very much in the manner of the old Roman sandal. The *cothurnus*, a high open-laced, boot-like sandal (shown on the Greek in the drawing) may be made in much the same manner by sewing duvetyne to the leather insole.

The Roman purple! Togas of the men may feature a border of this color six or eight inches in width. Conquering generals may wear a toga entirely of purple, with a border of gold. In fact, gold designs of crossed palms or other insignia may be added over the entire surface of the toga.

The graceful folds are the principal feature of both the Roman and the Greek costumes. Unfamiliar costumes of this type are hard to handle unless some practice is had. The wearer should experiment with handling the folds before venturing onto the stage. The costumes should be finished in ample time before the production so that young actors may have ample time to become familiar with their use and wear.

Greek costumes of the classical period are seen in the plays of the early Greek theatre, in Tennyson's *Princess*, in *Pygmalion and Galatea*, and the three following plays of Shakespeare: *Troilus and Cressida, Midsummer Night's Dream*, and *The Winter's Tale*.

Symbolical characters appearing in the Greek costume are Agriculture, Truth, and Loyalty. In addition, the costume is worn by interpretative or aesthetic dancers, in modification by fairy characters, and by the gods and goddesses of Greek mythology.

The heroes and heroines of the time are: Antigone, Achilles, Hector, Helen of Troy, and Paris. National characters are: Pericles, Socrates, Themistocles, and Plato.

Plays in which the Roman costume is seen are: *Coriolanus, Antony and Cleopatra* (Shakespeare's and Shaw's), and *Julius Caesar*. Symbolical characters clad in the Roman costume are: The Goddess of Liberty, Justice, and Eternity. Historical characters of the era are: Nero, Augustus Caesar, Caligula, and Mark Antony. The chief fictional character of the period is Ben Hur.

History books or pictures of the sculpture of the period are the chief sources of information about the costumes of the classical perid.

Costumes of the Middle Ages

The period roughly referred to as the Middle Ages covers a considerable length of time. Costumes varied at different times and in different countries. However, those to be used in most amateur plays follow rather closely those worn approximately during the period of the Plantagenets in England. With minor changes, the costumes described here may be used for any time during this period up to the Italian Renaissance.

The Men: The *surcoat* was worn by men. The surcoat, or surcote as it was known in France, was simply a long strip

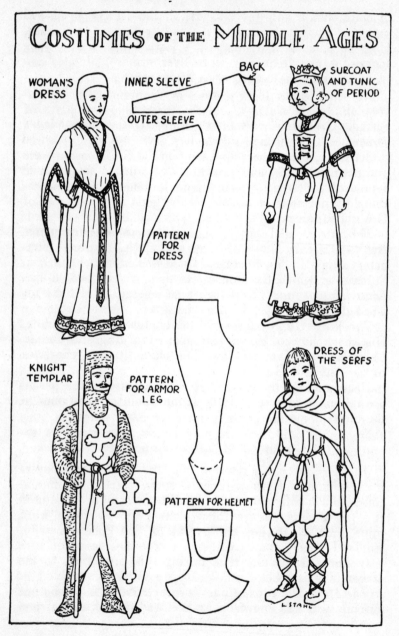

COSTUMES OF THE MIDDLE AGES

WOMAN'S DRESS

INNER SLEEVE

OUTER SLEEVE

BACK

PATTERN FOR DRESS

SURCOAT AND TUNIC OF PERIOD

KNIGHT TEMPLAR

PATTERN FOR ARMOR LEG

DRESS OF THE SERFS

PATTERN FOR HELMET

L. STAHL

of cloth with a hole for the head in the center. It slipped over the head and hung to the ankles in front and back. Held in place at the waist by a leather belt with a long tongue, it was frequently worn over armor and later emblazoned with the coat-of-arms of its wearer.

The king in the plate wears a long tunic under his surcoat similar to the long, loose garments previously described. The tight sleeves shown in the drawing are modelled somewhat after those of the modern shirt and may be sewed directly into the arms-eyes of the tunic at the shoulder without providing another garment. The tunic is edged with scraps of fur or embroidery dyed in imitation of the real thing by means of a brush.

With costumes of this type, both the surcoat and tunic may be made of duvetyne, though if a richer effect is desired and money is available, velveteen may be used. When using rough or "piled" materials of this kind, stencilled or brushed-in decorations are easier to apply if painted first on strips of sateen. It is then easy enough to sew the finished decoration to the garment itself.

The Women: The dress of the woman may be made of one of the cheaper grades of *panne satin*, sateen, or in case of a limited budget, even a cotton print will do. It is loose-fitting and held in place at the waist with a girdle. As with the costume for the men, it is only necessary to sew the second sleeve in with the first at the shoulder. The nun-like headdress, popular in some form or other during a great share of the Middle Ages, may be cut very much on the outline of the pattern designed for the helmet. White broadcloth or cotton will serve for the material. Again, it may be advisable to paint the embroidered decorations on separate strips of cloth before sewing them to the garment. Such a method has the additional virtue of allowing another contrast in the design by painting upon a second color of cloth.

Armor: The knight in armor presents a problem for the stage. It is possible to manufacture a fairly acceptable kind of plate armor out of papier mache, but this is a long and difficult process, therefore out of line for high school production. Armor plate can be rented, breastplates and such, but this is usually ill-fitting; the wearer looking like nothing so much as a misplaced furnace. For these reasons, armor of the chain-mail type is usually worn on the stage.

Embossed duvetyne is available from theatrical fabric houses purporting to represent chain mail, but at best, this material is not very successful. The best available substitute is a rough, knotty looking fabric known as mop cloth. Mop cloth is exactly what its name implies. It comes from dealers specializing in janitor supplies and is used for mopping floors! It is dyed to a middle gray by the costume shop. When cut and sewed, it gives a very acceptable imitation of chain mail providing a little aluminum paint is used for touching up here and there. For the latter, drag a half dry brush very lightly over the surface, hitting only the knots, to form highlights.

In case mop cloth is unavailable or hard to find, a coarse, gray rep may be used though this is not nearly so good as the above mentioned cloth.

Leg armor is made like tights, cut very similar to the legs in a pair of footed sleeping pajamas. The pattern shown in the drawing is for one front half. An identical pattern is reversed for the other leg and the heel cut off on the back half somewhat as shown on the dotted line. When sewed together, soles are added to the resulting tights by stitching in a pair of insoles from the ten cent store.

The upper tunic of mail is made like a modern shirt minus the tails. An old shirt may be used for a pattern. Mittens, with duvetyne palms, are made for the hands. Two pieces similar to the pattern are cut for the helmet with a hole cut in one for the face opening in front. In addition, an oval piece the size and shape of the head is cut and sewed in the top of the helmet to give it the necessary rounded shape. Two or three thicknesses of buckram may be used to stiffen this upper part of the helmet by sewing it inside in a band around the head. A Knight Templar, like the one shown, wears a white surcoat emblazoned with brilliant cross of red.

The Serfs: The dress of the serfs during this period of English history may be used also, with a little decoration, for the dress of the Saxons. A loose-sleeved tunic was worn with a cord knotted about the waist. Duvetyne may indicate the position of wealthier characters, but for peasants and serfs, ordinary burlap or baize will suffice. Loose-fitting tights can be made in the same manner as that indicated above for the armor and these fitted to the lower limb by means of cross-gartering extending to the knee. The same materials may be used for the tights as for the tunic.

Shoes may be simply woolen socks treated as described in the section of this book devoted to accessories. In addition, rough shoes for serfs may be fashioned by cutting a piece of duvetyne roughly to the shape of a large sole. Cord or straps of cloth can be fastened to this and the whole tied to the foot ending in the cross-gartering so common during the period. Ballet shoes will suffice for the women. Men of the richer classes can also wear the sheepskin shoes prevalent now with the turned-down tops. If these can be dyed a deep red or blue, so much the better.

During the latter part of the Middle Ages, tights became common. Allowances must be made for this development in costuming plays of a later period. When tights were worn, the tunic was shortened extending only to below the hips. It may be decorated in the same manner as previously described for the upper part of the costume remained very much the same.

History books and children's stories will furnish a wealth of ideas for costumes of this period. Illustrated editions of the stories of King Arthur, the novels of Sir Walter Scott, particularly *Ivanhoe*, or the tales about Robin Hood are all fertile fields in which to explore.

Prominent historical personages are: Richard, the Lion-Hearted, King John, Alfred the Great, Charlemagne, and Francois Villon. Costumes of the period are worn in any of the numerous plays about Robin Hood and the knights of old. In addition, such costumes are seen in many dramatizations of fairy tales such as the stories of Bluebeard and Cinderella. Variations of the costume are seen on pages and jesters and many gnomes. The costumes of the folk seen on our modern playing cards are directly derived from those of the Middle Ages.

The Elizabethan Period

The costumes of the Elizabethans are, perhaps, more common upon our stage than those of any other period. Shakespeare wrote his plays to be dressed in what for him was a contemporary style. We dress them so today. Then, too, the period itself has produced many stories and legends which have been woven into the dramatic literature of our time.

Clothing was very elaborate during the period of the Elizabethans; ladies and gentlemen of the court sought to outdo each other in fanciful array. Extensive padding of the costume made many men of the period resemble a pouter pigeon.

The Men: Men wore tights. A discussion of the alternatives that may be used in place of tights is contained in the section of the first chapter devoted to accessories. Beyond this, the most important item of men's dress is the *doublet.* It fitted the upper figure very closely, was tight about the waist, and featured rolls of *aiglets* (epaulettes) at the shoulders. The outer velvets of the costume were cut and slashed in regular designs, allowing the silken fabrics beneath to show through in what were known as "puffings". Puffings were used to decorate the breeches and even the shoes.

On the stage several satisfactory substitutes can be offered in making the costumes of the Elizabethans. In place of velvet, duvetyne or flannel may be used. Beads may be used to indicate jewels. Cheaper varieties of silks or satins will serve in the place of satins or brocades.

The doublet is cut somewhat like the modern shirt with the exception that it extends only to the waist and *darts* must be cut around the bottom edge of the material to make a snug fit. It buttons down the front with round gold buttons; hooks and eyes may be substituted if so desired.

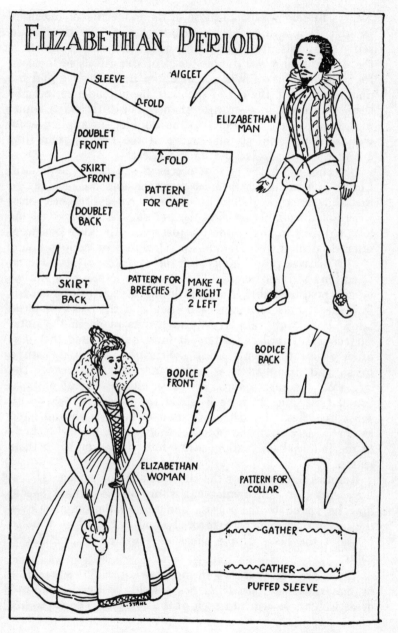

Elizabethan Period

SLEEVE

AIGLET

FOLD

ELIZABETHAN MAN

DOUBLET FRONT

SKIRT FRONT

FOLD

PATTERN FOR CAPE

DOUBLET BACK

SKIRT BACK

PATTERN FOR BREECHES

MAKE 4
2 RIGHT
2 LEFT

BODICE BACK

BODICE FRONT

ELIZABETHAN WOMAN

PATTERN FOR COLLAR

GATHER

GATHER

PUFFED SLEEVE

L. STAHL

Sleeves fit somewhat like those of the modern coat but more snugly. Before the sleeves are attached to the doublet itself, the aiglets are stitched in. These are cut as shown in the drawing and are double-faced of the duvetyne to make for added stiffness. When sewed into the arms-eye and the doublet is worn, the cut of the cloth has a tendency to make them stay erect in very nice shape. The little skirt, which may or may not be added to the doublet, is applied from widths of material slightly wider at the bottom than they are at the top to give the flaring effect.

Breeches are made of four pieces as shown in the pattern. Elastic is used in the hem at the waist and on each leg so that they may be puffed as desired. Knee breeches, also, were not uncommon during the period. These flared at the hips before clinging to the leg just above the knee and were often decorated with ribbons and slashings of various kinds.

The decorative slashings may be applied to the material from long strips of cloth. These may be either of a similar or contrasting color. An underlining of contrasting silk is first sewed loosely under each strip and the extra material allowed to "puff" slightly through cuts made in the outer surface. To simplify matters, it must be admitted that it is often easier to supply these contrasting slashings with a brush and dye than it is with a needle and thread. The strips of slashings may be sewed in either vertical or horizontal lines and may be used on the breeches, too. With short breeches, they often are used up and down and hang rather loosely from the breeches themselves, being "tacked" to the material only about every four inches or so of their length.

Rosettes are made for the shoes of silks or sateen. If costume shoes are not available, a short piece of black elastic may be sewed to the rosette and the whole snapped over the instep of a modern oxford. To add to the effect, it helps to paint the heels of the shoes a vivid red or some such color.

Capes are cut as shown in the drawing, a full semi-circle of material being used. Capes should be lined and lead dress weights sewed into each of the corners. The capes are attached to the shoulders by means of small loops passed over buttons sewed to the shoulders of the doublet.

The Elizabethan ruff is the important and characteristic feature of the costume. They were worn by both men and women, and at the height of the style, often attained a width as great as nine inches. Such were known as "cartwheels" and were suspended on elaborate contraptions of wire or bone. For the purposes of the stage, however, stiff tarlatane will serve well enough. A length of tarlatane in the required width is merely "gathered" and stitched into place around the neck. To avoid unpleasant chafing, tarlatane is rather rough, it may be necessary to stitch a narrow piece of smoother material around on top of the seam.

With all Elizabethan garments, it is advisable to make a lining of muslin. Linings help to give the requisite appearance of thickness and richness, and with the paddings of sawdust or bran so popular at the period, a good, stiff lining helps to give the appearance we so often see in the history books and paintings.

The Women: Important features of the women's costumes were the wide, flaring skirts held in position by *farthingales*, huge bone wheels suspended from the waist by ribbons under the skirt. The large puffed sleeves are typical, and the ruff, or the high, upstanding collar in back. Waist-lines were very small, frequently being confined in corsets of wood carved to form the fashionable figure!

Richest materials were in evidence. Silks, satins, and brocades were all used. To cut the cost, cheaper satins, sateens, or dyed muslin will do on the stage.

The tight-fitting bodice had a pronounced V-shape in front. The lining supposedly showed through as a sort of "gimp" in front, but for the stage, a contrasting piece of material may be sewed with considerable fullness into the "V" and held in place by the criss-crossed ribbons which lace on top of it. The sleeves are similar to those of the men except that they fit a trifle more tightly and may be cut with little tasseled V's at the cuff. The puffed sleeve is attached by gathering a piece of material shaped like that shown in the pattern. The top of the puff is sewed into the arms-eye along with the sleeve and the bottom directly to the sleeve itself. The open seam at the bottom of the puff may then be covered with ribbon or lace.

The high, upstanding collars are cut out of heavily starched lace curtains, or they may be made from two thicknesses of tarlatane. If the latter is used, lacy designs may be painted over the surface with white paint and a brush. In any case, the collar should be stiffened with a light framework of wire bound around its outer edge and one or two upright wires in back to keep it upstanding.

Make the skirt with an underskirt of muslin. Three widths of muslin will serve very well. In the front of the underskirt sew a panel of richer material to give the impression that the entire skirt is made of such finer stuff. The outer skirt is made of two widths of the material gathered in at the waist. It is open in front as shown to disclose the underskirt. For the amateur stage, if the skirts are sewed with sufficient fullness, the farthingales or other mechanical makeshifts to hold out the skirt need not be used.

For decoration, gold and silver ribbons or lace may be added to the costume or bead-work used to simulate jewels, providing, of course, that the beads are not too small.

The headgear of the Elizabethans was a hat very similar in shape to the one worn by the Pilgrim Fathers when landing at Plymouth Rock. Both men and women wore the same shape for outdoor wear. The man's hat being a trifle larger. Men wore their hats with a single feather for decoration while women had theirs decorated with medallions or jewels. Such hats for the stage are fashioned on a frame of buckram and covered with duvetyne or flannel in a color to match the costume or black.

The Servants: Servants, multitudes of which are seen in the plays of Shakespeare, may wear a simplified version of the costumes described above. Plainer materials are used, and there is little or no decoration. Men servants may not wear the doublet. Over the tights and breeches, a simple, smock-like blouse may be worn. Peasants of the time still wore the costume prevalent during the Middle Ages.

Typical costumes of the period are worn in Shakespeare's *The Taming of the Shrew*, *Much Ado About Nothing*, *Love's Labor Lost*, and *Othello*. Modern plays dressed in Elizabethan costumes are *Elizabeth, the Queen* and *Mary of Scotland*, both by Maxwell Anderson. Familiar characters besides Mary and Elizabeth are Sir Francis Drake, Shakespeare, the Earl of Essex, Sir Francis Bacon, Sir Walter Raleigh, and King James the First. The paintings of Rembrandt, Van Dyke, Holbein, and Rubens are loaded with costume ideas for the period. Sir Walter Scott's *Kenilworth* contains many references to the characters of the time.

American Colonial

Plays and pageants about our early history demand that the producer have some knowledge about what was worn during the early days of our country. Fortunately, a wealth of picture material is available, and from them, the prospective producer can gain a multitude of ideas about what to do.

Satins and duvetyne are materials for the stage, particularly in costumes for the men. Women may wear the lighter, more delicate cotton prints. Lace trimmings, so much a part of the period, can be cut from old window curtains. Even plain curtain material will do if the edges of the lace are *foliated,* that is, cut with fancy scallops to increase the lacy effect.

The Men: Breeches were tight-fitting and fastened below the knee with bands of the same material or ribbons tied into bows. For the stage, a band of elastic sewed into the top hem will serve to hold the breeches in place at the waist.

The coat is tight-fitting about the trunk and shoulders and flares out in the skirt below the waist. The pattern shows the cut of these coats and also the darts which must be taken in at the waist to give the correct fit. Sleeves are made like the standard sleeve with the addition of a broad cuff, often attaining a width of seven inches. Buttons were used extensively as decoration. They were sewed around the sleeves to hold the cuffs in place, across the flaps of the pocket, and very closely placed along the front of the coat.

Vests were long and hung down to below the waist. Cut like an abbreviated, sleeveless coat, they have darts front and back to give the tight waist. Small flowered prints may be used for the vests though a plain material will do. For best results, both coat and vest should be lined, preferably with heavy muslin except in those cases where the lining shows in the skirt of the coat. Here, a solid colored cotton print should be used.

Soldiers: The Continental soldier of the American Revolution wears a costume cut along similar lines. His coat must be of Continental blue, a kind of cobalt, slightly dulled. The coat is cut on the same general lines as the other except that additional material must be allowed in front and at the neck to make for the double-breasted effect. The front of the shirt on both sides is folded back, each corner meeting the folded corner of the slashing. Buttoned into position, these folds showed the white lining of the coat and allowed the soldier more freedom of movement. Swords are hung from a belt worn over the coat. Brass buttons are used and the epaulettes formed of gold cloth.

Cocked hats of the period are made on buckram frames. These are low-crowned affairs with a six inch brim. To give the typical tri-cornered effect, the brim, in three places, is merely "tacked" up to the crown. Ribbon may be sewed to the underside of the brim for decorative effect or small cockades may be used.

Stocks, the typical neckwear of the period, are merely white bands of cotton material fastened about the neck with either hooks and eyes or snaps. A white "dicky" may be worn down underneath the vest to indicate the shirt. On civilian dress, a lace frill is added.

The characteristic silver buckles on the shoes can be cut from silver cloth and sewed to pieces of black oil cloth cut to imitate the tongue. Black circular bands of elastic sewed to these will allow the wearer to slip them over a modern oxford in a manner very similar to that employed with the rosettes of the Elizabethans.

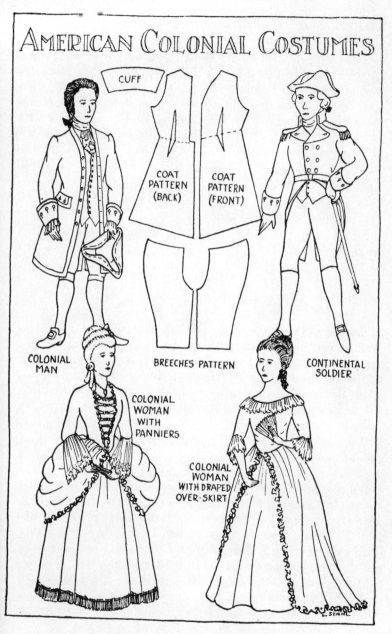

AMERICAN COLONIAL COSTUMES

CUFF

COAT PATTERN (BACK)

COAT PATTERN (FRONT)

BREECHES PATTERN

COLONIAL MAN

CONTINENTAL SOLDIER

COLONIAL WOMAN WITH PANNIERS

COLONIAL WOMAN WITH DRAPED OVER-SKIRT

L. STAHL

Opera hose in white are worn with men's costumes of the Colonial period.

The Women: In many respects, women's Colonial costumes resemble those of the Elizabethans. They have the same tight-fitting bodices with the point in front. Full skirts are draped open in front to show the underskirt. Sleeves were close-fitting, elbow length, and heavily trimmed with lace. As a matter of fact, ruffles of lace were common on all parts of the costume.

Soft cotton prints with small flowered designs or silkoline as used on comforters are excellent for this type of costume though silks and satins, or their stage substitutes may be used with good effect.

Skirts are made with two lengths of the material gathered in at the waist. The long, trailing overskirt shown on one of the figures is made of two and one-half lengths of the material cut longer in back to allow for the train. The overskirt is gathered principally in back from hip to hip to allow for the fullness.

Panniers, the heavily draped abbreviation of the overskirt shown on the other figure, are not so difficult as they appear. Two yards of the material in full width are draped across the back. The two bottom corners are then looped up to the front of the bodice and the remainder of the cloth stitched in place in such a way as to allow for the necessary fullness.

Wigs are essential with Colonial dress. If possible, these should be rented or cheap, serviceable wigs purchased if they are to be used again and again. White wigs of the Colonial period are often fashioned out of cotton batting, sometimes with sad results. If some such subterfuge is necessary because of the budget, better results will be obtained if the cotton is first stitched to a light, tight-fitting skull cap of cloth. Hair nets can then be worn over the wig to prevent any stray wisps of cotton from floating lightly down into the footlights during the big love scene. It should be remembered, however, that with Colonial wigs, the white, powdered variety were not worn during the period of the Revolution. The hair was left in its natural shade.

Should British soldiers appear on the scene, as they do in Shaw's *The Devil's Disciple,* their coats are of red. Their cut is similar to that of the coat worn by the American Colonial. More frequently, the British trooper wore boots reaching to the knees while the Hessians, as their distinctive insignia, wore a tall, mitre-like headdress shown in many pictures of the period.

American plays set in the Colonial period are *Nathan Hale* and *Rip Van Winkle.* English plays of like period are Sheridan's *The School for Scandal* and *The Rivals* and Goldsmith's *She Stoops to Conquer.* Familiar characters are Washington, Franklin, Paul Revere, and Betsy Ross.

Painters, reproductions of whose work form an excellent fund of source material, are Watteau, Reynolds, Hogarth, Gainsborough, Copley, Gilbert Stuart, and John Stuart Curry.

The Victorian Era

With the beginning of the Victorian Era, roughly the Lincoln Period in American history, the costumer may begin to search attics rather than depend entirely on skill. Styles, of course, changed and sometimes rapidly. Godey's *Ladies' Book* discloses that for every ten years or thereabouts a new silhouette was decreed. However, for the purposes of most amateur stage productions, one familiar costume can be made to indicate a considerable period of time.

For the women, this was the large, bell-like hoop skirt with tight-fitting basque, and for the men, the frock coat, tall hat, and the stock or Ascot tie. All costumes can, of course, be made by the costumer, but a diligent search will usually uncover something that is not only definitely usable but superior to what can be made on short notice.

The Men: Frock coats can be cut on a pattern similar to that shown for the dress of the Colonial period. The skirt is less full, the cuff is trimmer, and the coats are most often double-breasted. The lapels are trimmed with silk or satin. Waistcoats are cut like a modern vest and may be either white, tan, or flowered. Trousers are made of duvetyne, light tan or buff and not too full. Cuffs were not worn on the trousers and the bottom often fastened under the instep with a band of elastic.

Shirts oftentimes featured a ruffled front. Ties, in the early part of the era, were the broad, black stock of silk as shown in the drawing. Later, the black Ascot tie or the black string tie were very good.

The tall hats so fashionable at the time are made of black duvetyne covering a buckram frame.

The Women: Hoop skirts require a bit of doing, but they are not beyond the abilities of the amateur costumer if a little ingenuity is used. First, a cloth band is fastened tightly about the waist. From this, about eight long streamers extend to the floor with several inches to spare. Progressively larger wire hoops, four in number, are suspended from the streamers and sewed in place. On the

THE VICTORIAN ERA

PATTERN
FOR SKIRT
OF COAT

finished hoop, long valances of lace are sewed around on the inside to protect the modesty of the wearer in case she loses control of the frame while sitting down.

Five and a half straight widths of the material are required to make a skirt. It is gathered in fullness about the waist. Sateens may be used. Decorations were elaborate; at one time, every available inch of the skirt being covered with flowers, drapery loops, and *passimentaries*, glistening works of embroidery, fashioned out of small beads.

The tight-fitting basque waist or bodice may be cut from a pattern greatly resembling that used in the previous period.

In contrast to the gathered fullness of the skirt, the light coat worn over the dress for street wear was smoothly fitting. For this reason, the skirt of the coat must be made of six shaped panels cut as shown in the drawing. The sleeves of the coat were wide and full, extending to slightly below the elbow. Like the dress, the coat was elaborately trimmed with surface designs.

Hats were rather small; the poke bonnet was popular, though many women wore the large picture hat when it first began its long reign of favor. In either case, the hat was secured by a long black ribbon fetchingly tied underneath the chin. Usually, the costumer will be able to find a hat of the period to serve as a model. This should be done if possible.

Colors were rather subdued. Black was very popular as were the deeper shades of green, purple, or wine, though young girls often appeared in the paler shades of yellow, green, or orchid, and often in white.

In the event that hoop-skirts or the bustle, which appeared later during the period, are impractical on the stage, a compromise can be worked. Reasonably full skirts can be cut out of four lengths of the material and given a somewhat wider effect through wearing a number of stiffly starched petticoats underneath. This obviates the necessity of the wire frameworks which are often awkward for the inexperienced to handle.

Pantalettes, those little modesty pieces of women's attire, appeared somewhere around the beginning of the reign of Queen Victoria and were mostly *passe* by the time Lincoln became president. They were not full-length, but fastened above the knee with elastic bands. A second elastic bound the pantalette around the ankle. The bottom was trimmed with a ruffle of lace.

Plays employing the Victorian costume or versions of it are:

A Christmas Carol.	*Young Lincoln.*
David Copperfield.	*Mignonette.*
Oliver Twist.	*Little Women.*
Silas Marner.	*Disraeli.*
The Hoosier Schoolmaster.	*Abraham Lincoln.*
Jane Eyre.	*Barbara Freitchie.*
Beau Brummel.	

Novels with scenes laid in the period are:

Vanity Fair.	*Pride and Prejudice.*
Henry Esmond.	*Lorna Doone.*
Gone with the Wind.	*Uncle Tom's Cabin.*
The Crisis.	

Prominent personages during the Victorian Era are:

Lincoln.	*Disraeli.*
Clay.	*Gladstone.*
Webster.	*Queen Victoria.*
Calhoun.	

John Singer Sargent was the most prominent of the portrait painters of the period and his work is filled with many ideas for costumes.

The Gibson Era

Many styles have flourished from the dawn of the Twentieth Century to our own day. One need only compare the

dress of the present with that of ten or even five years ago
to see the difference.

However, for the purposes of the stage, we can well restrict ourselves to a period running very roughly from 1900
to 1910. This was the height of the Gibson Era, so named
after Charles Dana Gibson, an artist by that name, who
created "the Gibson girl."

The Women: Women's figures as revealed in their costumes were rather trim compared to what they were in the
previous period. The skirt fitted the figure rather closely
until it flared at the knees. Trains on the skirt were popular
and were carried in the hand by means of a small loop
when walking or dancing. The shirtwaist was rather full
and "bloused" in front, an effect to be seen in most of the
pictures of the time. The leg-o'-mutton sleeve also had its
day during this period and was made very similar to the
puffed sleeve of Elizabethan times though of lighter material. The "Merry Widow hat", so named after the popular
light opera of the day, was the most common type of headgear for women. It was a large, flamboyant affair with
several plumes.

The Men: Men's costumes began to resemble more
closely those worn by the male sex of the present day.
Trousers were tight-fitting. The peg-topped trouser, tight
at the ankle and calf, but flaring out at the hips, was often
seen. Coats were either single or double-breasted and cut
very like those of the present day. Sometimes the skirt
was rather short, the coat extending to very little below
the waist. The lapels in front had a tendency to stay up
rather high around the neck. The vests, too, had lapels very
much like those of the coat. The derby hat, in brown,
black, or gray, was the popular type of hat for men.

All of these costumes, or suitable substitutes, can usually
be uncovered by a diligent search through family attics.
There is scarcely a village or hamlet in America which
does not have its full quota of such costumes stowed away
somewhere in a battered trunk. Usually, it will be easier
to find women's costumes than it will be those of the men,
but with a little cutting and snipping, men's discarded suits,

THE GIBSON ERA

even of the present day, can be turned into fairly exact replicas of costumes worn at this time.

Plays employing the costumes of the Gibson Era are:

Huckleberry Finn.   *Giants in the Earth.*
Huckleberry Finn, Detective. *Ah, Wilderness.*
Garden of the Moon.   *Cavalcade.*
Smilin' Through.   *Garden of the Moon.*

Dance Costumes

There is no standardized costume for the dance except the familiar flounces of ballet. Costuming may be anything that the dance or setting requires. Naturally, because of the movement, dance costumes must be made so the legs and arms are not restricted in any way.

Many effective dance costumes can be built on the basis of the *leotard*, a knitted garment which closely resembles a one-piece bathing suit. As for instance, a skirt and brief bolero may be added to the leotard and the costume for the Spanish dancer is complete.

Other costumes, suitable for the modern jazz dance, require short trunks and a bodice or jacket, the latter tight-fitting. One version of this costume is illustrated in a form suitable for a jockey dance. If so desired, in place of the jacket, a tight-fitting bodice with short, puffy sleeves can be substituted, notably for such types of dancing as the jazz toe.

Ballet skirts are of two kinds: The short, extremely full type with row and row of tarlatane, and the longer, in some respects, more graceful type. Both are made by sewing length on length of the tarlatane round and round the bottom of the bodice though the skirt and bodice can be made separately if so desired. Tarlatane is sewed with the width of the material going the long way of the skirt and gathered into tiny folds as the work proceeds. Afterwards, the bottom edge of the tarlatane may be cut with points or scallops to give a softer effect.

To relieve the solid white of such costumes, the skirts are often appliqued with little designs in gold or silver. In fact, entire costumes are often made in the pastel shades of pink, light blue, pale green, rose, or orchid. Tarlatane may be obtained in these colors.

Leotards are best purchased from the theatrical or dance supply houses though they can be made from knitted cotton, silk, or rayon. They come in a wide variety of colors. Tights may be used in many dances. The cheaper cotton ones can often be purchased.

Special dancing shoes, the ballet slipper, the acrobatic shoes, and the musical comedy shoe with large "theo" are all best purchased from dealers specializing in this business, though acceptable versions of the latter can often be made by lacing light oxfords with wide ribbon.

Designers planning dance costumes need not restrict themselves to the fabrics found in other costumes. Novelty fabrics of all kinds, capable of many striking effects, are offered by the dealers listed in the back of this volume.

DANCE COSTUMES

Unless one knows what the market affords, many exciting possibilities in dance costumes are apt to be missed. Some of these novelty fabrics are very reasonable in price and "closeout" sales may make them more so.

Common costumes which are adaptable to dancing in addition to the ones described above are: The classical dress of ancient Greece; the sailor suit in blue or white; the various peasant dresses similar to the Hungarian and Swedish national costumes, and the abbreviated versions of the full evening dress for men with top hat, white vest, colored trunks, and "spiked" coat.

Fairy Costumes

Fairies, sprites, brownies, and gnomes of all kinds and description make their appearance in the annual school May Fete and in many plays for younger children. Considerable imagination may be employed in costuming these little creatures of the woods and fields. There are wood fairies, flower fairies, wood gnomes, water sprites, a host of others, and each one should betray in his costume his dominant love or characteristic.

Fairy queens may be effectively garbed in a white cheesecloth version of the Greek chiton. The chiton may be trimmed with golden stars. To give the regal effect, the queen wears a little coronet or crown of gold and carries a wand.

The fairy king may also be dressed in glistening white, but his costume more closely resembles that in vogue during the time of the Elizabethans. He may wear a short cape. His crown is of gold and the white of his costume may be relieved with trimmings of gold.

Fairies of this kind must wear wings. These are constructed on wire frames. The wire (about 20 gauge) is bent to the shape of a butterfly wing and sewed to the back of the costume at the shoulder blades. The surface of the wings may be formed by cheesecloth, light gauze, or cellophane. Dyed designs may be added to show the veining of the wings.

The typical costume for a brownie can be made of brown duvetyne or plain cotton print. Tights are worn. The upper part of the costume is formed by a short tunic with rather full sleeves. For best effect, these sleeves and the bottom of the tunic are foliated or cut in scallops.

The brownie hat is a perky affair made after the style of hat worn by Robin Hood and his merry men in Sherwood Forest. Pieces are simply cut in the shape of the hat and sewed together. It lies flat when not worn very much in the manner of the "overseas" hat adopted almost universally by the American Legion. It achieves its distinctive shape when worn on the head.

Water sprites are dressed in blue, fire sprites in red. The spirit of the harvest wears golden yellow, the spirit of spring light green. Autumn appears in reddish brown, the color in each case explaining the character of the spirit or sprite.

The basic costumes described above can be cut to emulate further the character of each and every sprite. Fire will have his dress cut with long, pointed streamers to indicate flames. Jack Frost may similarly be garbed in white. The spirit of the harvest, may wear a mantle cut roughly into the shape of husks about the ear of corn.

Flower fairies of various kinds are most easily indicated by using a robe of light green or green. A large ruff of tarlatane, cut to resemble the wanted flower, is worn about the neck. In addition, the entire costume may be cut to resemble a flower. The long, flowing mantle is cut into petal shapes as was done with the corn.

Costume ideas for fairies and spirits may be liberally obtained from the numerous illustrated editions of children's story books. The number is legion, and most of the costumes will adapt themselves very well to the materials the costumer finds to be ready at hand.

Nationality Costumes

The national peasant dress of various countries is gradually fading out of the picture, but on the stage, especially in operettas, they are often seen.

Many times the peasant dress seen in stage productions is not particularly accurate. There has come to be a sort of standard costume to indicate peasants of many types. The costume used is roughly a variation of the dress worn by the peasants of the Black Forest and undoubtedly receives its inspiration from the fact that many early operettas were laid in this country.

With this costume, women wear a rather short but full skirt of bright color decorated with contrasting ribbons above the hem. Over the white blouse, a laced *kirtle* similar to the Elizabethan bodice is worn. It is in black or colors. On her head, the peasant woman wears a lace cap greatly resembling an old-fashioned sunbonnet and a bright shawl is pinned around her shoulders. The stockings are white and the low-cut shoes have buckles of silver. Colors are all very bright and frequently the apron, always worn with the costume, or the blouse and skirt are profusely decorated with embroidery.

The typical man's costume is cut somewhat on the lines of the Bavarian costume or the dress of the Tyrol. Short breeches, worn with wide, embroidered suspenders, are the distinctive part of the dress, such breeches ending just above the knees with little ties, rosettes, or bows. Shirts are of white cotton and have large, flowing sleeves ending in a tight cuff at the wrist. Coats, though short, may be cut very much on the lines of the Norfolk jacket popular for outdoor wear not so many years ago. White stockings and buckled shoes may be worn, or in the case of the mountaineer, heavy woolen stockings in bright colors may reach to the knees with heavy, spiked brogans upon the feet. Hats are very similar to the Tyrolean hat now being worn by men on sporting occasions.

The Dutch Costume: The loose, baggy trousers worn by Dutch men and boys are familiar to everyone. In addition, a tight-fitting, double-breasted vest is worn with a shirt or a short jacket cut very much on the lines of the vest. A stock is tied about the neck like a modern scarf. Dutchmen may wear a round cap of fur or a little fez-like head-

NATIONALITY COSTUMES

TYPICAL PEASANT COSTUME

DUTCH GIRL

DUTCH BOY

SPANISH

BAVARIAN OR ALPINE COSTUME

piece with a tassel down the back. Duvetyne is excellent material for making the costumes of Dutchmen and boys.

The dress of the Dutch women and girls is very like that of the peasant costume previously described except that more lace is used in place of embroidery. The distinctive lace cap is made somewhat on the order of paper "soldier hats" with wires inserted to hold out the wings on each side.

Wooden shoes, without which no Dutch costume can conceivably be complete, are best bought or rented though they can be made in the manual training shop with a draw-knife and chisel if sufficient skill is available. Also, fair models of wooden shoes can be made of papier mache, but these are very unsatisfactory; they have the bad habit of falling apart or cracking when least expected.

The Spanish Costume: The dress of Spanish women, beyond its more flamboyant coloring, is very similar to that worn by the women of other countries. The distinctive feature is the *mantilla,* a black lace veil draped over a comb in the hair and hanging down the back nearly to or shortly below the waist.

With the men, many compromises can be worked. Corduroy slacks, worn by college and high school youths everywhere, make excellent trousers providing they are slit a trifle up the outside seam and a colored gore inserted. With Spanish men's dress, black Tuxedo trousers may also be worn. The shirts are white with very full sleeves bound at the wrist with a cuff. Short embroidered bolero jackets are very much in order. The typical Spanish hat may be closely imitated by taking a straw sailor and blacking it thoroughly with enamel. The little balls, so distinctive a part of the hat's trimming, are stolen from old portieres. With all Spanish men, except those of the very richest classes, a long blanket or mantle in bright colors was carried draped across the left. It was used as a coat and often allowed the poorer wearer to curl up anywhere for his daily siesta.

In England and on the continent, it should be remembered that peasant dress as a whole did not change as rapidly as did that of the ruling classes. Men working in the fields wore a costume until a very late day like that employed during Anglo-Saxon times, a short blouse, with rough breeches and leggings bound about the calf with strings and leather thongs very much like the cross-garters of old. Women wore simple smock-like dresses with kirtles, the inevitable white cap of lace, and shawls. With this work dress, the prevailing colors were dull greens, deep browns, and gray.

Plays and pageants in which the national dress of various countries is worn are: *Marcheta, Sweethearts, Autumn Crocus, The Windmills of Holland,* and *The Toymaker of Nuremburg.* From time to time, *The National Geographic Magazine* publishes excellent series of plates depicting the national festive dress of various countries. These can be studied to good effect.

Chapter IX

COSTUMING THE MODERN PLAY

The costuming of the modern play requires as much thought and care for success as does the period play. It is, perhaps, even harder to control, for the costumes are not assembled in the costume shop. Instead, Mary insists on wearing the new "formal" which she purchased for the "prom", or Bill, playing the father, possesses only one suit of bright green color and sees no way to borrow another. Or again, there is no available dress for gangling Ruth who must find something to fit her and still suggest her mother role.

Problems of the Director

In the first place, the director of the play must be the complete dictator. She must wield her power in this matter even as ruthlessly as do a Hitler or a Mussolini.

Her problem will be greatly facilitated if she works out a tentative costume chart detailing the colors and types of costume needed for each character. Shortly after the cast is chosen, she may meet with each individual member and the costume committee to discuss very carefully the needs in costume. The costume committee can then make arrangements to borrow whatever is needed.

Each member of the cast should be given a list of what he requires and duplicate lists should be given to the committee. Also, it's a very good idea to post another list on the bulletin board where it may be seen in case some list is lost. These lists should include every article of apparel, gloves, purses, hats, and caps, even though the script may not indicate the need of them. Nothing is more disconcerting to an audience than to see a character walk in from the street without a hat. Admittedly, college boys do not wear hats, but our businessmen do!

The matter of appropriate costume in every detail is something else that should be considered. The authors well remember a memorable performance in which the girls of the cast all decided to wear their formals. Very pretty it was, too. The only drawback: The scene was laid on a Sunday morning and all the characters were returning from church! Another thing: boys when first appearing in evening dress often make the mistake of wearing white socks with their Tuxedos or checked ones, enough to make the *bon vivant* scream with pain. Details like this should be watched and carefully checked.

Clothes should be comfortable; this goes without saying. It is very difficult for an actor to appear at ease when he may be made wretched by his clothes.

Care should be taken to see that all the men appearing in the play do not wear the same color in their suits. A surly father and a happy-go-lucky son should offer as much contrast as possible in the way of costuming; sweaters and slacks serving for the son while the father appears in a business suit of severe coloring and cut. Gray suits may offer a contrast with blue suits, or browns with tans. On one occasion, the authors dressed a peppery old grandfather from Samoa in a white linen suit. The spot of white offered exactly the right note of contrast and effectively spotlighted a most important character against the rest of the cast.

The tie is important, bright ties being worn by young heroes and those of exuberant personality while the more quiet characters appear in sombre hues. In fact, the tie, which is the modern male's only dash of color, is one of our vital means of showing character upon the stage.

While on the subject of men's suits, a boy playing the part of an older man should wear a suit which is a trifle too large for him. The suit should be cut on more elderly lines. Nothing suggests youth more than those belted-back models which are so popular at the present time. A bath towel or two wrapped about the waist and securely pinned will help to suggest more weight and age if desired.

A young girl can suggest a middle-aged woman more easily by wearing a large-sized corselet with a layer or two of cotton wadding sewed to its inner surface. An extremely old woman may be suggested by wearing a shawl and pulling it up in folds about the shoulders to give the appearance of a hump. Padding may be stitched across the back of a high-necked waist to form rounded shoulders. Another simple device which proves effective in suggesting age is a black velvet or satin band worn about the neck up under the chin. The neck is where age first shows in women.

Occupation also has a great deal to do with what the character will wear in a play. All farmers do not dress alike, but the straw hat, blue denim overalls, rough shirt, and red bandana handkerchief dangling from the hip pocket immediately suggests the rural character. The painter is known for his white overalls, the mechanic for his greasy looking coveralls in striped gray or khaki, the artist for his smock and tam. All these are typical costumes and suggest to the audience a great deal about character before the wearer even speaks.

Changes in costume also observe the same consistency. The farmer may change from overalls to Sunday suit, but it is inconceivable that his Sunday "store" clothes will look a great deal like those worn by a Miami Beach millionaire. Neither will Aunt Polly, in the last act of *Huckleberry Finn*, appear in modern sport clothes after having been seen in the first two acts with a bustle and old-fashioned lace mitts.

Men's Formal Dress

Throughout the amateur play world, there prevails the greatest confusion of ideas as to what men may wear for formal dress. The wearing of white or colored socks with a Tuxedo has already been mentioned. Women, usually, have a fairly accurate idea of what to wear, but men, with very definite conventions of what is correct at the right time, often go astray.

On very formal evening occasions, the *full* dress suit is obligatory. In other words, the Representative Extraordinary of Plotz-Pilsen will not appear wearing a Tuxedo. The Tuxedo is for a less formal affair, more suited to the cocktail party and night club wear than it is to an ambassadorial reception.

Men's full dress include black trousers, spiked coat, white vest, and white tie. Black pumps of calf or patent are worn. The silk hat is obligatory. In this country, the Chesterfield, a simply cut overcoat, is worn for outer wear, while in Europe, the Inverness cape, with white satin lining, is still rather popular.

The Tuxedo has black trousers with braid or black satin at the outer seam similar to the full dress coat. The coat may be either single or double-breasted. A black bow tie is worn. Vests are most often of black silk, satin, or grosgrain, though lately, white vests of pique are often worn. Contrary to popular opinion, the Tuxedo is not correct for weddings. Evening weddings demand the full dress suit.

Daytime or formal afternoon wear is also strictly conventional. The ambassador or man-about-town appears for an afternoon tea wearing gray-striped trousers, cutaway coat of black or dark gray, black shoes, white linen spats or those of pearl gray, and the top hat or a derby, the former preferable. The black Ascot tie is looked on with favor for this type of costume or gray or black four-in-hands in stripes or Paisley designs may also be worn. Lately, however, it must be admitted the black, Oxford gray, or dark gray suit coat cut on conservative lines may also be worn as formal afternoon dress by younger men. White gardenias are popular for the button-hole and gray gloves are worn. This dress is correct for afternoon weddings.

Esquire, the Magazine for Men, and the national arbiter of what is correct in men's formal, will gladly answer any queries with the receipt of a stamped, self-addressed envelope for reply.

With business and and sport clothes, the average boy has enough familiarity to preclude the necessity of discussing it here.

Butlers and Servants

Butlers and men servants in the homes of the wealthy have as strict a convention of dress as do their masters. For the butler or houseman, a white coat is perfectly permissable while doing the morning's work, but while serving, or in the afternoons, a more formal attire is demanded.

The butler's afternoon wear resembles the formal dress of the man, but a black vest and a black bow tie is always worn. Neither does the butler wear spats with his gray-striped trousers and cutaway coat. For evening, the butler wears the full dress suit with *black* vest and *black* bow tie to distinguish him from any guests who may be arriving. The black and yellow striped vest so often seen on stage butlers is not exactly correct. Properly speaking, it belongs to the costume of the footman.

Chauffeurs and liveried footmen may wear anything that the heart of their employers so desires, but the most typical chauffeur's uniform is in gray or drab green. A uniformed cap is worn together with a Norfolk and either trousers or breeches and puttees. Footmen may wear a uniform similar to the full dress suit in colors like dark blue or green. Oftentimes, for decoration, the uniform is edged about with contrasting piping.

Confidential servants, secretaries, and the like, wear cloth at all hours of the day like that of their employers though the cut and color of the costume is usually more modest.

In modern costume, as with everything concerned with the stage, good sense must be used. The hired girl with a farm family is not going to appear in the black sateen uniform, white apron, and cap that distinguishes the maid in the homes of the rich. Appropriateness is the one key that opens the door to success in costuming for the modern stage play.

Chapter X

BIZARRE COSTUMES

Many of the costumes contained in this chapter are not, strictly speaking, costumes for the stage. They are included in this book because high schools frequently find use for them either at carnivals, parties, on national holidays or for other events.

The costumer will do well to explore further the field of materials available for costumes of this type. In addition, to the muslins, duvetynes, and sateens so often mentioned, there are cheaper and more unusual materials that will find a use.

First among these is *paper cambric*. This is a cheap, rather sleazy material generally unsuitable for stage use, but for party costumes, it can be used. *Crepe paper,* too, can be utilized for making party clothes. The Denison Company, manufacturers of crepe paper supplies, issues a splendid volume describing the method. Novelty materials, such as oil cloth, cellophane, or animal cloths (produced by the stage fabric companies) can also be used in making bizarre costumes. Even newspapers have been used with good success in certain cases.

Clown: Everyone is familiar with the baggy, loose-fitting clothes of the clown. The pattern shows the *right front* section. The bottom of the sleeves and breeches may be cut as shown or left straight and gathered into fullness around the wrist and ankle. In any event, the costume should be left as loose and free as possible to allow for plenty of movement.

They are usually white. If white is used, trimming is done in red, blue, or yellow, narrow *pipings* of *bias tape* being sewed around the edge of the ruffs. With *parti-colored* clown costumes, each half of the front and back sections

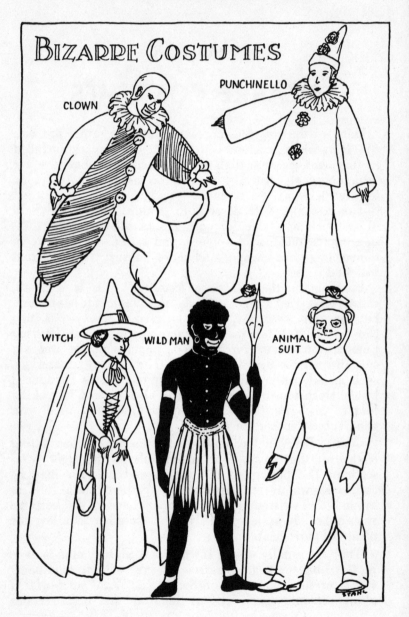

are cut from different colored material, either green and yellow, red and blue, yellow and violet, or some such combination.

Muslin may be used for the material, but paper cambric has been worked up into very acceptable clown costumes.

Ruffs for the neck, wrists, and ankles may be fashioned either of like material or tarlatane, already familiar from previous use, may be employed in a manner similar to that of the Elizabethan costume. The skull cap in white, so familiar a part of the clown costume, is sewed from white *jersey*, generally a part of an old, discarded undershirt.

Wild Men: The "Wild Man of Borneo" makes his appearance in the high school carnival or in the "prom" based on the jungle theme.

It is totally unnecessary for him to "black" the greater portion of his body. A union suit is worn, one that has previously been dyed to the color desired. The grass skirt is made of yellow paper cambric or cotton print. Several thicknesses of the material are first sewed into the skirt and the body of the skirt then shredded with a scissors. It fastens about the waist with an elastic band.

The face and hands are covered with minstrel black or burnt cork, a comedy Negro wig is used, and the jewelry applied by resurrecting a number of the brass curtain rings used in hanging up draperies. The wild man is all ready to frighten his public.

Harlequin: The costumes of the Italian *commedia 'dell arte* are still seen upon our stage today. Harlequin, Polichinelle, and Columbine are nearly as familiar to people now as they have been to audiences in centuries past.

Polichinelle, or Punchinello as he is more commonly called, wears sateen or muslin. His costume resembles nothing so much as an over-blown pair of pajamas with very full legs and sleeves. The addition of pom-poms forms the decoration. These are usually of tarlatane, either in black or colors, with a single length of the material gathered into a puffy ball.

Black "sneakers" or tennis shoes are worn on the feet. The addition of a pom-pom on an elastic band will add to the appearance. Tall, peaked hats will require a buckram frame underneath the muslin or sateen, but very often, Punchinello wears nothing but a white or black skull cap fastening with loops under the ears like that of the clown.

Columbine, or Pierette as she is known in France, wears the costume which has been adapted into our modern ballet, the tarlatane skirt and tight-fitting bodice previously described in the chapter devoted to dance costumes.

The costume for Harlequin is a bit more difficult to accomplish as it must be skin-tight in fit. Cheap white tights may be used for the lower portion of the costume. For the trunk and arms, it may be possible to obtain a "T" or training shirt with wrist length sleeves, or sleeves may be sewed out of jersey to one with quarter-length sleeves. The patch-work effect in diamond shapes applied all over the costume is done with a brush and dye, in greens, blues, violets, and yellows. Harlequin's headwear is usually a black skull cap and he may wear black sneakers on his feet.

Animal: The beasts of the jungle often make their appearance at costume parties or as characters in fairy plays or pageants. They are not so difficult to make as they seem.

For the bodies, fur cloth may be purchased from the theatrical companies, but these are quite expensive and school use often does not justify the outlay. For ordinary purposes, the materials mentioned so far, sateen, cotton, duvetyne, or even burlap, may be used to good effect.

The bodies are made like pajama suits, loose-fitting, and of the appropriate color for the particular animal desired. Mittens of like material are worn on the hands and an elastic band usually passes under the arch of the foot to hold the trousers in place. The distinctive feature of any animal costume is, of course, the head. Make a tight-fitting hood with shoulder piece very similar to that shown for the knight in armor previously described. When the hood is worn, a mask, purchased cheaply for the occasion, may be "tacked" in place around the face opening. Tails, if necessary, are attached by sewing on a piece of rope covered with cloth of the desired color.

Stripes or other peculiar markings can be applied to the costume with dye.

Witch: The witch costume, familiar as a part of our celebration of Hallowe'en, follows very closely in pattern the typical peasant dress described earlier. It has the bodice or *kirtle* tightly laced across the waist, but the skirt is usually longer. In addition, the witch usually wears a long, flowing black cape which floats behind her as she rides the broom on her midnight rides and a tall, peaked hat fashioned on a buckram frame. Her magical powders are carried in a pouch at her side.

Witch costumes need not be black, though they usually are, sateen being used. Relief may be applied to the costume by making the kirtle of some other color, dark green or purple. Sometimes also, mystic symbols in white or silver are sewed to the costume, stars, moons, or suns. In any event, variations for numberless witch costumes can usually be found by exploring through the pages of children's books.

The Devil: Mephistopheles, as he is more commonly known, is familiar to us from Gounod's opera, *Faust.* He is clothed in red, usually silk or sateen.

In outline, the main body of the costume is identical with that described for the men of Shakespeare's day. He wears the doublet, breeches, and tights. In addition, a long, slithery cape hanging from the shoulders and reaching to the floor is worn. In place of the ruff, he wears a collar, a high upstanding affair constructed on lines similar to that described for women of the period. A hood is worn. This is cut and sewed identical with other hoods except the face opening has a pointed tab hanging down on the forehead in front to give that sharp-featured appearance so desirable in a character of this type.

Symbolical Characters: It happens that the costume maker will sometimes be required to make costumes for such characters as Jack Pumpkinseed in *The Wizard of Oz* or a character having a square head or some other such distorted feature.

The matter is not so difficult as it sounds. First, make a framework of fairly stiff wire in the shape desired and cover this with cloth. Use ten or twelve gauge wire for the framework itself and bind the pieces together wherever necessary by using a lighter stove-pipe wire. Wear and tear can be avoided on the outer cloth by first winding the wire framework with narrow bands of muslin.

Besides those mentioned, our American holidays oftentimes demand a type of costume that will frequently be used in high schools. Though they cannot, strictly speaking, be called bizarre, nevertheless, they do have a place in a book of this type.

Santa Claus: The costumes seen on the jolly saint of Christmas are often a poor substitute for what might be done. One good costume, well made and well taken care of from year to year, will give much more satisfaction than a makeshift assembled from odds and ends each time it is used.

The basis of the costume may be duvetyne, in red. The white fur trimming may be either flannel, duvetyne, or if money is available, the white knitted stuff sold under the name of *angora*. The belt and boots for Santa are made of black oil cloth, and of course, the costume must be large enough to allow for a liberal stuffing with pillows.

Santa Claus masks are available to cover, but at best, these are very poor. They hide all expression on the face. It is better, by far, to choose as Santa some person with a full, round face and accomplish the rest with make-up and a manufactured beard and moustache.

Pilgrims: Costumes of the American Pilgrim Fathers in numerous Thanksgiving pageants are too well known to need description here. However, it may be said that the ever-faithful duvetyne, in dark gray, serves very well here. Hats are made on a buckram frame for the men while the women wear the little white banded caps so familiar with the pictures. In every respect, the costumes are made in the manner described for similar dress.

Indians: Indians appearing in high school pageants or plays usually wear a great deal more clothing than was

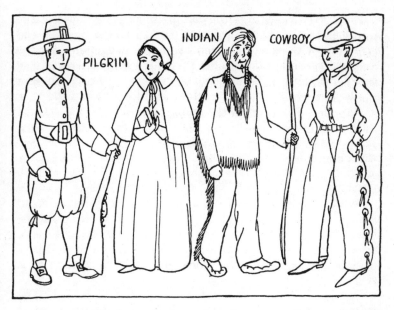

customary with the red man when he was at home. Breech clout and leggings marked the costume of the brave when he was on the warpath, but for all school purposes, it will be much better to make the Indian costumes somewhat like the play suits worn by small children.

The superior material is duvetyne in a buckskin shade. A plain, simple dress with beaded decorations will do for the women while men wear a pair of trousers and a shirt. They are made rather full. An added four inch strip may be sewed into each seam when the costume is put together and this allowed to show on the outside. It can be cut like a buckskin fringe and the bottoms of the garments cut to represent the fringe in like manner.

Strings of beads, large wooden ones are best, may be worn around the neck, but for application upon the costume itself, work with a brush and the dye-pot gives the best effect.

Cowboys: The chaps are the one part of the costume that will have to be made. Simply take a strip of brown or tan colored duvetyne and sew it to the front of each leg on a pair of old overall pants. The outer edges should be scalloped or fringed. A nice effect entails the use of *nail cleats,* used in fastening roofing paper to walls, along the outside seam. These are sewed in place at the center of each scallop with a narrow strip of the duvetyne knotted in place on each cleat.

Complete the costume by using a large felt hat, shaped as shown in the drawing, a blue or brighter colored shirt, and a large silk bandana around the neck.

Chapter XI

FIRST STEPS

The Make-Up Kit

The beginner need not purchase a large and elaborate make-up kit to get started. He may follow either one of two methods: he may purchase one of the beginner's kits especially prepared by the cosmetic companies offering stage make-up, or he may assemble his own kit as needed.

There is considerable variety in the assembled kits offered by manufacturers. The Stein Company has a splendid assortment of grease paint sticks in a little tin box though it is necessary to purchase powder and cold cream separately. A more expensive kit, but a very complete one, is offered by the publishers of this book.

For the beginner who wishes to assemble his own kit, the following articles will be necessary: One box or jar of cold cream, two or three sticks of foundation grease paint (See appended list), three or four sticks of lining color, one box of a neutral theatrical face powder, two powder puffs, stumps for lining color (Orange wood sticks, toothpicks, or match sticks may be used), and a cosmetic brush, which is not strictly necessary but very convenient. In addition to these items, a jar of moist rouge and a box of dry rouge may be added. The wise beginner will also provide himself with a fair-sized towel and a box of cleansing tissue for removal of the make-up and to keep his clothing from becoming soiled while he is working.

The following list shows the best of the colors to buy:
For Men—

STEIN'S	MAX FACTOR'S
Grease Paint	*Grease Paint*
4 Juvenile Flesh	3 Juvenile Flesh
7 Light Sunburn	3½ Sunburn
27 Cinema Yellow	26 Panchromatic
Lining Colors	*Lining Colors*
7 Dark Brown	2 Dark Brown
9 Medium Blue	16 Medium Blue
14 Vermilion	9 Maroon-Crimson
15 White	12 White
Face Powder	*Face Powder*
No. 8 Tan	8 Outdoor, Neutral
Moist Rouge	*Moist Rouge*
3 Medium	3 Medium
Dry Rouge	*Dry Rouge*
14 Twilight	18 Theatrical

A stick or tube of Olive grease paint may be added to any one of the above selections.
For Women—

STEIN'S	MAX FACTOR'S
Grease Paint	*Grease Paint*
1 Pink	2 Pink
7 Light Sunburn	3½ Sunburn
13 Olive	5A Olive
Lining Colors	*Lining Colors*
7 Dark Brown	2 Dark Brown
9 Medium Blue	16 Medium Blue
14 Vermilion	9 Maroon-Crimson
15 White	12 White
Face Powder	*Face Powder*
4 Flesh	6 Naturelle
Moist Rouge	*Moist Rouge*
3 Medium	3 Medium
Dry Rouge	*Dry Rouge*
No. 18	12 Light Theatrical

It should be understood that an ironclad selection cannot be given. Some effort should be made to match the complexion as experience dictates.

With the above equipment and a little practice, the beginner should be able to accomplish a wide variety of "straight" and character make-ups.

GENERAL METHODS

The Base

The face is prepared for make-up by covering it with a thin layer of cold cream. The cold cream fills up the pores, assists in the removal of the make-up, and makes a smoother *base* on which to work.

Dip the fingers in the cold cream and cover the face, neck, and ears with a succession of light dabs. *Do not* use too much. If the face becomes too greasy, if too much is used, the excess should be carefully wiped off with a towel or cleansing tissue before proceeding with the make-up proper.

Foundation Tints

Foundation tints are applied with grease paint. They form the "foundation" on which the highlights and shadows are applied.

Grease paint comes in two varieties: A fairly stiff variety which comes in sticks and a "soft" paint available in tubes. The first is applied by smearing the grease paint lightly over the face, the neck, and the ears, the second by covering the face, neck, and ears with a succession of tiny dabs.

Then, with the fingers, the grease paint is spread evenly over the face, neck, and ears until a smooth, even foundation is achieved.

Be careful that the foundation is not too heavy. If it is impossible to see the natural pores of the skin underneath the foundation, too much has been applied and some of it should be removed.

The choice of grease paint will depend entirely on the type of character being portrayed. Youth will require a robust tint, old age a more sallow color. Degrees between the two may be achieved by blending two or more foundation tints directly on the face, that is, a light grease paint may be smeared over a darker one and the two tints blended directly on the face.

In another blending method, and a very popular one, a little cold cream is smeared in the palm of the left hand and the two foundation tints are blended there, then applied to the face. This latter method allows the beginner to gauge the tone of the blend before it is applied to the face, but the first method is less troublesome.

The important thing is to have a smooth, even foundation tint over the entire face, the neck, and the ears.

The Cheeks

The natural blush of the cheeks may be supplied with a ruddy (Sunburn) grease paint, moist rouge, or a Carmine, Scarlet, or Crimson lining color. With all these colors, the important thing is the blend. The color may be quite bright or high in the center of the cheek area, but it must blend or shade imperceptibly into the surrounding foundation tint.

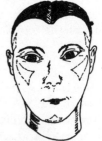

STAHL

NORMAL FACE   BROAD FACE   LONG, NARROW FACE

FIGURE 1   CHEEK COLOR

Most amateurs use too much color on the cheeks. The color should never be obvious as such. It should merely remove the flat and otherwise pallid complexion of the face.

Cheek rouge is applied to an area roughly triangular in shape. If a bright cheek rouge is used, it may be applied in a small circle on the point of the cheek bone and blended with the thumb to the position indicated (See Fig. 1). A duller color may be applied in this position before being carefully blended with the foundation tint. There should be no sharp edges around the rouge on the cheeks. It is desirable to have a smooth, even flow of color blended from the foundation tint into the high point of color on the cheek bone or below it.

In youth, the color is high on the cheeks, around the cheek bone. In old age, the color has a tendency to sink lower down the cheek. This fact should be borne in mind.

Also, a round, broad face may be narrowed somewhat by bringing the cheek rouge in closer to the nose and dropping in somewhat lower on the face. Conversely, a long, narrow face can be broadened by keeping the cheek rouge high on the face and working it outward away from the nose.

Commonly, in straight make-ups, the cheek rouge is lightly blended upward to give a faint blush to the temples. Cheek coloring naturally does so in a healthy character, and the practice has a tendency to enhance the sparkle of the eyes. Do not overdo it, however. Color on the temples must be very faint.

The Eyes

The eyes are the most expressive feature of the actor's face and care should be taken in making them up, or they may resemble the proverbial "holes in the snow."

The eyes are shaded on the upper lids. The simplest method proceeds as follows: Apply a dark blue lining color in a roughly triangular shape on the upper lid (See Fig. 2). Apply a touch of Vermilion or deep red in the inside corner just where the nose joins the forehead bone and on the outside of the eye on the prominent bone just under the brows. Then, with the index finger, carefully blend the two colors together, working in from the vermilion and out from the blue. The color should shade from a dark blue in the center, through violet, and out to a light Vermilion at the outer edges just under the brows.

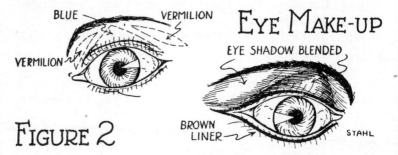

FIGURE 2

The brows are next heightened with lining color in the appropriate shade applied with a stump or orange-wood stick, though a specially prepared eyebrow (Dermatograph) pencil may be used for this purpose.

A thin, narrow line of brown liner is next applied with a toothpick or orange-wood stick both above and below the eyes just next to the lashes. The two lines join at the outer edges of the eyes and may be extended out about a quarter of an inch. Care should be taken so these lines are not too heavy nor wavering. A thin, neat line gives the best effect. Use a toothpick or a match whittled to a point for the best results. The average make-up stub is too blunt for this type of work.

Quite frequently, mascara is also added to the lashes in the make-up of the eyes, especially with women. This is done with a little brush provided for the purpose. Its use is not recommended for men on the stage.

On occasion, a small red dot is added on the inside and the outside corners of the eyes to brighten them but this little fetish may well be dispensed with by the modern make-up artist. However, it does no harm.

The Nose

A smooth, regular nose requires no special treatment. Foundation tint is applied as on the other portions of the face, but an irregular nose may be straightened through the use of make-up.

To straighten a crooked nose, a straight line of white lining color is drawn directly down the center and blended lightly into the foundation tint. The irregularities on each side of the nose are then touched with a light blue or gray shadow to make them less prominent.

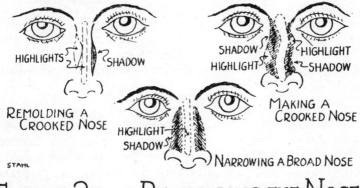

Figure 2a   Re-shaping the Nose

The same process is reversed in forming a crooked nose. An irregular line of highlighting is drawn down the bridge of the nose and corresponding highlights and shadows blended into the foundation tint to give the appearance of irregularity (See Fig. 2A).

The Lips

Do not use too much rouge on the lips; a deep red gash across the face should be avoided. Middle-aged or old-aged characters need not use rouge at all.

Women may make up their lips with the rouge that best suits their complexion. For young men, the use of a ruddy (Sunburn) foundation grease paint is recommended.

Lip rouge is applied with the tip of the little finger. Care should be taken to make the lips as symmetrical as possible. A small mouth may be lengthened by extending the lip rouge to the farthest limits of the mouth, a large mouth may be shortened by carefully keeping all rouge away from the ends. The lower lip is never as bright as the upper one. A too pronounced, impossible "Cupid's bow" should be avoided as the plague.

The Chin and Ears

A spot of Dark Sunburn grease paint or a tiny dab of moist rouge is placed on the upper rim of the ear, the lobe, and on the point of the chin. These are blended into the foundation tint. Further than this, no special attention need be given these features except in character make-ups.

Powder

It is not necessary for the beginner to burden himself with innumerable boxes of make-up powder. A neutral shade (Stein's No. 8) will do for the men while a Light Pink (Stein's No. 2) will do for the women. As progress is made, a box of Olive or Sunburnt powder may be acquired and this blended with the lighter color to form any number of shades.

Use powder freely. It should be liberally applied to the face with a puff, allowed to set for about thirty seconds, then carefully removed with a cosmetic brush. Such a procedure prevents that greasy appearance which is the result of careless make-up.

Make-Up Removal

Make-up is removed with the use of cold cream. A dab is taken on the end of the fingers and patted over the face. Work the cold cream into the grease paint thoroughly by massaging the face with the fingers. Remove with a towel or cleansing tissue. If one attempt does not remove all the make-up, repeat the process until the face is clean.

Modern theatrical make-up material is absolutely harmless. Its use need not be feared in any way though but, of course, reasonable care should be taken to keep it out of the eyes. Make-up will enhance the complexion, not harm it, if it is thoroughly removed each time it is used.

Chapter XII
THE STRAIGHT MAKE-UP

Straight make-up is presumed to be that which does not alter the shape or appearance of the character's face. It merely counteracts the effect of stage lighting and increases the visibility of the actor's face at a distance. However, with perfect propriety, it may be used to improve the appearance of the actor's face, make it more symmetrical, reduce objectionable features, and enhance attractive ones. As one professional actor put it, "I may not be able to act, but I at least can look my best!"

The beginner should preface a study of make-up with a study of his own face, learn its bad points and its good ones. Then, with proper practice, he can learn to make himself up more effectively.

Straight Make-Up (Male)

Pale Juvenile: This type of make-up is suitable for the average type of indoor male until approximately the age of thirty-five.

Materials needed—

Grease Paint: Pale Juvenile, Dark Sunburn.

Lining Colors: Medium Blue, Light Brown.

The foundation tint of Pale Juvenile is applied exactly as prescribed in Chapter 1. Dark Sunburn grease paint is used in place of rouge on the cheeks and around the eyes. Medium Blue is used for the shadows of the eyes. Light Brown is used in lining the eyes. The eyebrows may be heightened in either brown or black depending on the color of the hair.

Juvenile Robust: The materials needed are essentially those employed in the lighter make-up. It is only necessary to blend a bit of the Sunburn grease paint into the paler juvenile to give it a ruddier color. Dark Brown may be used for lining the eyes. If, after applying the Sunburn to the cheeks, they are not ruddy enough, they may be heightened by adding a bit of dry rouge to each cheek *after* the make-up has been powdered.

It will be seen from the foregoing that straight make-ups are not difficult after the general method has been mastered. The chief rules: avoid elaborate detail; do not use too much.

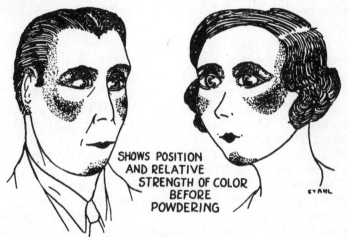

SHOWS POSITION AND RELATIVE STRENGTH OF COLOR BEFORE POWDERING

FIGURE 3   STRAIGHT MAKE-UPS

Straight Make-Up (Female)

Blonde Make-Up:
   Materials needed—
      Grease Paint: Light Pink.
      Lining Colors: Blue-Green, Carmine, Light Brown.
      Face Powder: Light Pink.
   The foundation tint of grease paint is applied as previously described. Cheek and lip rouge is supplied with the Carmine lining color or a light shade of moist rouge may be used. The shadows above the eye are made by using the Blue-Green and the Carmine as described in Chapter 1 in place of the Blue and Vermilion. The Light Brown is used for the lines along the lashes and for the eyebrows.

Brunette Make-Up: This make-up is not essentially different than the one described above except that a darker foundation paint (Juvenile Flesh) may be blended with the Light Pink. A Dark Blue lining color is substituted for the Blue-Green, and a darker moist rouge (Medium) may be used for the lips and cheeks. In most cases, however, the Carmine lining color will be found quiet sufficient for the lips and cheeks.

Sun Tan Make-Up: Vigorous, outdoor types will on occasion demand a ruddier make-up than the ones just described. This can be accomplished by brushing the first powder off the make-up immediately after it has been applied and powdering again with a deeper shade (Olive). This method results in a smoother make-up rather than applying the olive-tinted powder directly to the grease paint. The powder may be heavily applied for a brunette type and lightly dusted over for a blonde.

Society Make-Up: In high school productions, the question frequently arises: How to make a young, immature girl appear like a sophisticated society person? This can best be accomplished by eliminating the cheek rouge entirely. The lips are made brighter and just slightly more full. The method is most successful when employed with dark-haired persons or platinum blondes. It is not to be recommended with medium blondes. The method is most effective on paler types of make-ups, although it can be used with a Sun-tan make-up. It all depends upon the character and the locale of the play. Sometimes, the quantity of cheek rouge can be retained in the Sun-tan make-up, but its use should be restricted and the color should be kept relatively high on the cheek.

Chapter XIII
BASIC CHARACTER MAKE-UPS

The face is made up of a series of planes. These planes are formed by the skull and the muscles which cover it. When the sculptor models the human head in clay, the contours of the face are blocked out with these planes clearly visible. By working from these basic planes, the sculptor can be sure that he is retaining the essential character of any face.

The Sculptural Method

The make-up artist will find his work greatly simplified if he, too, works on a system of planes. The reader is referred to Fig. 4. As the sculptor applies clay or scrapes it away to achieve a distinction in facial character so the make-up artist raises or lowers these separate planes.

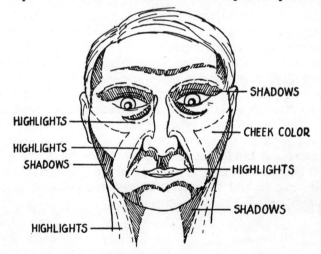

HIGHLIGHTS

HIGHLIGHTS

SHADOWS

HIGHLIGHTS

SHADOWS

CHEEK COLOR

HIGHLIGHTS

SHADOWS

FIGURE 4 - THE SCULPTURAL METHOD

Planes are lowered in facial make-up by applying shadow: Blue, Gray, or Lavender. They are raised by highlighting in white or light yellow. Such a make-up can be made more convincing and real than anything accomplished under the older method of covering the face with lines supposed to be wrinkles. The method follows the course of nature in allowing the flesh to sag at the approach of old age and is the easiest, most effective way of converting a bright young high school person into a doddering octagenarian.

At the approach of old age, the flesh sinks on the temples, over and under the eyes, around the mouth, on the cheeks and around the neck. These are the important areas to be kept in mind when making up for old age.

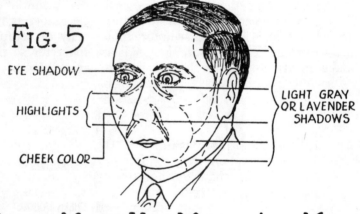

Fig. 5

EYE SHADOW ——

HIGHLIGHTS {

CHEEK COLOR ——

LIGHT GRAY
OR LAVENDER
SHADOWS

Basic Make-Up ~ Middle Aged Male

Middle Aged Make-Up

The make-up for middle age is one of the most difficult to accomplish. A young person can quite successfully be made into an old-aged character, but it takes more skill to represent the attributes of middle age.

Until the age of forty, it is best to make no strong attempt at character make-up. Until that age, a slight shadow under the eyes, a bit of gray hair at the temples, and, perhaps, a strengthening of the lines around the mouth should be deemed sufficient. In any event, strong, violent lines should never be used in a make-up of this type.

Basic Male (Pale) :

Materials Needed—

Grease Paint: Motion Picture 27 (or its equivalent), Dark Sunburn.

Lining Colors: Medium Blue or Gray, Vermilion, White, Light Brown.

Foundation tint is supplied by the Motion Picture 27. (This is Stein's make-up. No lip rouge is used. Dark Sunburn grease paint is used for the color on the cheeks. It should be remembered that the cheek color is placed somewhat lower on the cheek in a character of this type (See Fig. 5).

Shade the eyes on the upper lid exactly as described for the straight make-up. Then, with a stump or orangewood stick, take the Medium Blue or Gray and draw lines lightly under the eyes as shown and in the heavy indentation that extends from the nostrils to the eyes. The blue above should be blended carefully up toward the eye; the blue below should be blended down toward the mouth. After this is done, dip the stump again in the Vermilion and draw again over the blue with a fairly light line of Vermilion. This color is carefully blended into the blue until the shadows take on a violet or lavender tint. Next, on the projecting bone that comes down from the nose just under the line previously drawn, place a line of White (or Yellow). Do the same *above* the line on the nose. Likewise, this highlighting should be carefully blended into the foundation tint, downward around the eye and upward and outward on the line around the nose. Care should be taken to follow the natural contours of the face in doing this work.

The next step consists of sinking the cheeks and the neck a little bit although this may be done before the lining colors are applied. With the blue or gray (preferably gray) place a very light tint from the hair line just in front of the ear down across the cheek to the chin being careful to follow the natural outline of the beard. This should extend down the neck to the collar line. It should be done very lightly and smoothly so as to avoid any unkempt appearance. The area to be shaded is shown at the side of the face in Fig. 5. It follows the natural line of the beard.

The eyelids and brows are lined with Light Brown and the make-up powdered as before. In addition, the hair may be grayed across the temples or completely (depending on the character) by using ordinary corn starch and a powder puff or white mascara.

Basic Male (Robust): There is only one essential difference between this make-up and the one described above. A little of the Dark Sunburn grease paint is blended into the foundation tint before the rest of the work proceeds.

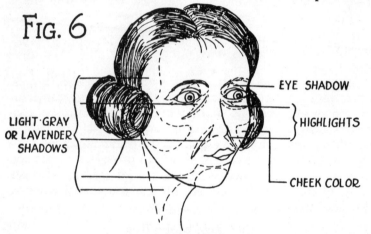

FIG. 6

LIGHT·GRAY OR LAVENDER SHADOWS

EYE SHADOW

HIGHLIGHTS

CHEEK COLOR

Basic Make-Up   Middle Aged Female

Make-ups like the above are frequently enhanced by the addition of beards and moustaches. These refinements will be discussed in the next chapter.

Basic Female: Middle aged make-ups of this type sometimes require little more than the graying of the hair. Women, because of the greater care they give their faces, frequently do not show their age as rapidly as men.

Materials needed—
    Grease Paint: Pink or Light Pink, Dark Sunburn.
    Lining Colors: Medium Blue or Gray, Vermilion,
    White, Light Brown.

Pink or Light Pink serves as the foundation tint. The Dark Sunburn grease paint may be used for cheek and lip rouge. It should be remembered that the cheek rouge is carried lower on the face as in the male make-up.

The eyes are shaded above exactly as in the straight make-up. In addition light shadows are placed below the eyes as described in the basic make-up for the male. The use of gray or blue on the cheeks is to be discouraged. These colors, however, may be used on the neck in a roughly triangular area bound by the lower line of the jaw, the "Adam's apple," and the heavy muscular cord that runs upward from the breast bone to behind the ears (See Fig. 6).

It is only fair to say that with some middle-aged female characters it is not necessary to use the lighter grease paint on the cheeks and lips. If they are the type who use cosmetics, the regular moist rouge may be used. The cheeks should be made up more heavily in these instances than they would be in the case of youth, to provide contrast and to heighten the sallowness of the rest of the face. Proper study of the character will tell the make-up artist when to do these things and to what degree.

Old Age Make-Ups

Before starting an old-aged make-up the artist will do well to study his own face carefully and turn again to the chart contained in Fig. 4. He should decide which areas on his own face correspond to the planes on the chart before making up his mind which areas on his face he wishes to shade or highlight.

Roughly, the sunken areas are found at the temples, under the eyes, around the mouth, and on the cheeks and neck. The highlighted areas are usually next to these for the sake of contrast.

Basic Male:

Materials Needed—
　　Grease Paint: Motion Picture 27, Dark Sunburn or Light Sunburn.
　　Lining Colors: Medium Blue or Gray, Vermilion, White.

Fig. 7

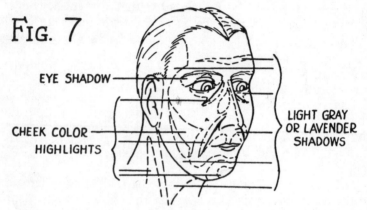

EYE SHADOW

CHEEK COLOR
HIGHLIGHTS

LIGHT GRAY
OR LAVENDER
SHADOWS

Basic Make-Up ~ Old Aged Male

As in the middle-aged make-up, use the Motion Picture 27 for foundation tint. The color on the cheeks is supplied with the Dark Sunburn and placed very low (See Fig. 7). The sunken areas are next outlined with the blue or gray. These must all be carefully blended into the foundation. Above, on the temples and the side of the forehead, it is well to blend in a little Dark Sunburn to give these areas a violet tinge. Highlight the areas under the eyes and around the nose as was done with the middle-aged make-up. In addition, highlighted areas must be supplied around the mouth as shown in the drawing. Apply shading above the eyes as was done in the straight make-ups and with the middle-aged make-ups.

Do not use lines around the eyes or the brows, nor use mascara of any kind, nor lip rouge. These things are all unnecessary. The simpler make-ups depending principally on lights and shadows are the most effective.

When the make-up is completed, the hair may be powdered with corn starch to give the final touch of age.

It will be noted immediately that this type of make-up does not employ any of the favorite fetishes of the old school, the crow's feet in the corners of the eyes, the heavy lines across the forehead. Experience has shown that these things are unnecessary under the conditions of modern stage lighting. If a certain number of wrinkles are required, they may be supplied with an ordinary soft lead pencil after the make-up has been completed. For lines on the forehead, a favorite method entails the use of an ordinary rubber comb. The forehead is contracted and the back of the comb drawn through each wrinkle. The effect is satisfactory under modern stage lights.

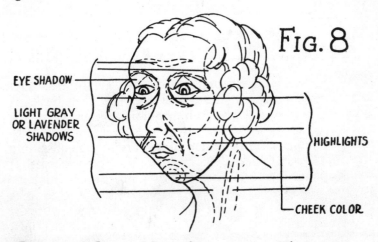

FIG. 8

EYE SHADOW

LIGHT GRAY OR LAVENDER SHADOWS

HIGHLIGHTS

CHEEK COLOR

BASIC MAKE-UP ~ OLD AGED FEMALE

Basic Female: The materials used are the same as employed in the middle-aged make-up. The general method of using them is identical with that employed for the male make-up. Effects are more subtle and greater care must be exercised in blending the make-up on delicate complexions.

It should be remembered that all the effects outlined for these make-ups are only basic. They may be enlarged or eliminated entirely in special cases. Again it should be said: the wise make-up artist will study his own face and the character which he aims to play and adapt any given method to the circumstances.

Chapter XIV
AIDS TO CHARACTER MAKE-UP

With the simplified make-ups in vogue today, special care should be given to the choosing of accessories, costumes, etc. It will be the purpose of this chapter to outline the many features that may be added to the grease paint make-up.

Crepe Hair

Crepe hair is customarily available in the following shades: White, Light Brown, Medium Brown, Dark Brown, Light Gray, Dark Gray, Auburn, Blonde, and Black. The color of the wearer's hair should not 'be matched exactly, but in a lighter shade, as crepe hair has no sheen, and on the stage, appears somewhat darker than it really is.

Crepe hair comes in a tightly twisted braid. For best success, the crepe hair should be washed to remove the wrinkles before it is used. This is done by cutting off a convenient length (about six inches) and swishing it about in water until the curl is almost completely removed. It is then hung up to dry. The curl may also be removed by pressing it out with a damp cloth and a hot iron.

The hair is applied to the face by using spirit gum. Spirit gum, when it comes from the manufacturer, is rather light; its adhesive qualities are poor. It will be best to leave the bottle standing open a day or two before using to encourage evaporation and stiffening. Such a precaution will eliminate the unhappy possibility of having a moustache float lightly away in the midst of an important scene.

After the crepe hair is washed, it is combed with a coarse comb until the bundle of hairs lie flat and straight. It may then be cut with a scissors to any shape desired and applied with the spirit gum.

Moustaches: Apply spirit gum to the upper lip in the

shape desired. Then, with the scissors, cut out the crepe hair to the desired shape of the moustache and press it firmly in place using the index finger.

BRUSH TYPE   WAXED TYPE

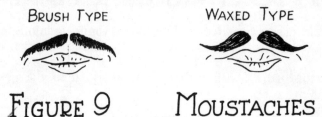

FIGURE 9   MOUSTACHES

There are two principal types of moustaches, one in which the hair grows downward (the "brush" type), and one in which the hair grows outward away from the nose to a little point at the end. The distinction is made in the cutting of hair, by either cutting against or with the grain. In the latter type, the point on the end may be obtained by applying a little spirit gum and twisting it into shape with the fingers exactly as if moustache wax were being used.

The thin, hair-line type of moustache so frequently seen is sometimes drawn in place with a lining color although crepe hair may be used.

When the crepe hair is firmly in place, it should be neatly trimmed with scissors unless the moustache is to be one of the unkempt type. In any case, it will be wise to trim the hair away from the mouth and nose to avoid the unpleasant sensation of tickling.

Beards: Beards are built up by applying successive pieces of crepe hair until the whole is completed. It is best to build a firm foundation for the beard by painting the required portions of the face with spirit gum, then covering this area with finely cut crepe hair. When this is fairly dry, another coat of spirit gum is applied and the beard put in place.

All beards are built merely by enlarging on the method used in the formation of a goatee. A piece is cut as shown in Fig. 10 and placed on the upper portion of the chin, being careful to press it firmly around the bone. A similar piece is then applied to the bottom of the jaw, and smaller, narrower pieces applied to each side to form the body of the beard. A tiny piece is placed above the beard to connect it with the lip as shown and a succession of smaller pieces used on each side to build it along the side of the jaw.

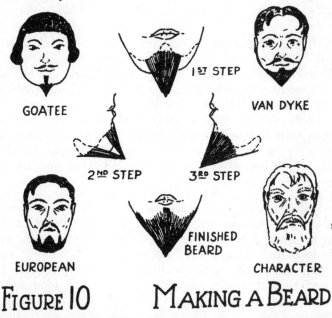

GOATEE   1 ST STEP   VAN DYKE

2 ND STEP   3 RD STEP

EUROPEAN   FINISHED BEARD   CHARACTER

Figure 10   Making a Beard

The larger, Imperial type of beard, and the full beard are built in exactly the same way except that more and larger pieces are used in the making.

It is well to remember one or two points: As far as possible, the beard is kept away from the mouth to leave this expressive feature free. The hair is kept rather sparse underneath the jaw and always pointing outward to support the beard. Such a method of placing the hair under the jaw has the added virtue of avoiding friction with the collar or coat.

Naturally, after the crepe hair has been applied, the

beard should be neatly trimmed with the scissors. If a point is desired on the end, it may be supplied by applying spirit gum and twisting the hair in shape.

Manufactured beards are available on gauze foundations. The shorter types may be used in cases of emergency, quick-changes, etc., though the average make-up artist will want to use his own. In cases where long, chest-length beards are desired, it is safest to use these made-up beards. They may be made more natural looking by applying crepe hair lightly around their edges after the beard is put on.

More or less permanent crepe hair beards to be used on successive occasions may be made by the make-up artist himself. The jaw is rather heavily coated with cold cream and a heavy foundation of grease paint applied. Ordinary mucilage is then applied to the face in place of spirit gum to hold the crepe hair. When the mucilage is dry, the beard may then be removed from the face and used several times by re-applying it with spirit gum.

Sideburns: Sideburns are built up by using a modification of the method employed in making beards. Spirit gum is applied to the areas required and the sideburns built from the bottom up. The successive layers of crepe hair are about a quarter inch in length. Of course, for heavier sideburns, or muttonchop whiskers, longer hair must be used at the base and tapered off to join the hair at the temples. In emergencies, light sideburns may be painted on with lining color or an eyebrow pencil.

Rough Whiskers: Frequently required for tramps or similar characters. For this effect, crepe hair is simply cut into short lengths and applied where the beard would naturally be. Spirit gum may or may not be used depending on the length of the hair.

In removal, the crepe hair is jerked quickly from the face. The residue is removed with cold cream and warm water and soap. If the beard proves stubborn, a little alcohol will aid the process.

Nose Putty

Nose putty is used to change the contours of the face, the nose, the jaw, and in application of warts, cauliflower ears, and other blemishes. Its use is not recommended wherever it can possibly be avoided. It is stiff and unyielding and spoils the expressiveness of the face.

The nose putty is moulded in the hand until it becomes soft, and spirit gum applied to the feature where it will be used. When the spirit gum is nearly dry, the nose putty is applied and moulded until it has the shape desired. Grease paint may then be applied over the nose putty exactly as on any other portion of the face though cold cream is not used on the putty; it becomes too greasy and soft.

Wigs

Wherever possible the use of wigs should be avoided. The hair should be dressed in the style desired. When wigs are essential there are several points that will aid the make-up artist in their use.

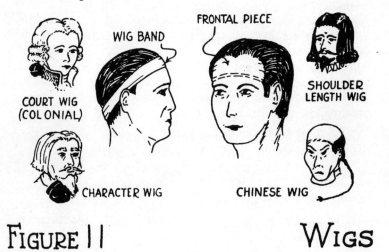

COURT WIG (COLONIAL)

WIG BAND

FRONTAL PIECE

SHOULDER LENGTH WIG

CHARACTER WIG

CHINESE WIG

FIGURE 11   WIGS

More success will be obtained if a "wig band" is used. This is a light band of gauze about an inch and a half wide which is tied firmly around the head. The wig is held in place by fastening it to the wig band with hairpins. Wig bands are not needed with the female wig or *transformation*, if the wearer's hair is luxuriant enough to hold the pins.

The most troublesome part of any wig is the band of cloth which so often extends across the forehead. This type of wig should be eliminated whenever possible, but when its use cannot be avoided, it may be treated somewhat as follows: Make certain first that the cloth is clean, then glue the lower portion of the frontal piece to the forehead with spirit gum. The juncture between the cloth and the forehead may be made less obvious by coating it heavily with the foundation tint or by smearing nose putty thinly across this line. The patented preparation, "Nu-Skin," (collodion) is sometimes also used for this purpose. The entire frontal piece of the wig is then covered with grease paint until the cloth is invisible.

The wigs used in most amateur productions are usually rented. They may be ill-fitting and none too clean. A too large wig may be tightened somewhat by stitching it up on the inside with a needle and thread until it fits snugly. This may best be done over the ears and across the back. Wigs are cleaned by washing them thoroughly in a pail of kerosene or dry cleaning fluid. Afterwards, they should be hung up to dry and brushed out thoroughly by placing them on a wig block until they possess a glossy sheen. There is nothing more unnatural looking than a dirty, crumpled wig.

Make-Up of the Hair

The manufacturers of theatrical make-up offer various preparations for graying the hair, white mascara and while liquid powder. These may be used with perfect safety, but for ordinary amateur purposes, white corn starch serves as well and is less expensive.

Corn starch is applied with a powder puff. It may be used over the entire head or just along the temples and a little gray lock above the forehead. The effect of a wave may be imparted to hair grayed in this manner by removing a portion of the corn starch with a comb in imitation of the waves.

Brown or blonde hair may be made black through the use of black mascara. A hair brush is dipped in water, then in the mascara and brushed across the hair. Care must be taken not to get the mascara too heavy around the edges of hair; otherwise, the method results in a highly artificial appearance.

On occasion, the hair may be turned to red or auburn shades through the use of grease paint or lining colors. A little cold cream is rubbed into the hair. Then, grease paint of the required shade is mixed with cold cream until it attains the consistency of paste. The resulting mixture is brushed into the hair. It must be said, however, that this latter method is not recommended unless it is absolutely unavoidable.

Mascara or grease paint in the hair should be removed immediately after each application to prevent unnecessary drying or stiffening of the hair. Warm water and soap will accomplish the task.

Eyebrow Changes

The shape of the eyebrows may be changed by plastering down the original brows and drawing the new ones over them in the desired shape. The plastering may be done with a thick layer of grease paint, nose putty, or common soap. With the latter two methods, the foundation tint is placed right over the eyebrows before lining the new ones in the desired shape.

The effect of bushy eyebrows may be obtained on eccentric characters by applying spirit gum to the brows and adding short lengths of crepe hair. It is used most frequently on hags and witches and older men.

Miscellaneous Effects

Scars and Bruises: Ordinary surface scars may be painted on the face by using lining colors, blue, red and yellow. They are more effective if a little white is added for highlighting effect. Flat surface scars or bruises may cover a wider area and the edges are blended into the foundation tint.

Ridges or welts on the face may be built up first through the use of nose putty and then painted with the colors described above.

Indentations in the face may be indicated either through the use of collodion or by smoothly spreading nose putty over the surrounding area and indicating the scar by indenting the putty with a stump or lining stick.

Black eyes come under the heading of bruises and should be painted around the eye with the colors described above. Every effort should be made to give the black eye a natural appearance. It should not be too dark.

The Teeth: Teeth are blacked out with the aid of a black tooth wax specially made for the purpose. The wax is chewed to the proper consistency and then molded over the teeth with the fingers. Black lining color may be used also if all moisture is carefully wiped from the tooth before it is applied.

Blood: The appearance of blood on a character is simulated by mixing red or carmine lining color with cold cream until it has the consistency of thick cream. It is then applied to the face or hands as desired.

Freckles: Brown or Light Brown is merely daubed on the end of a stump or make-up stick and applied in dots where wanted.

Costume Accessories

When young people are appearing in the parts of older persons, spectacles should be worn whenever possible to increase the effect of age. Horn-rimmed spectacles, glasses with frames and bows, *pince nez,* or glasses of the Oxford type will all help to distinguish the character.

Monocles may more easily be kept in the eye by painting their edges with spirit gum before they are inserted in the eye.

With men, care should be taken in the choice of neckties. An older man may wear a white linen tie or a black string tie. The flowing Windsor tie has long been symbolic of the artistic type of character. The Ascot tie will feature the morning dress of Englishmen or foreign diplomats. All of these things should be studied when working on the character.

Women in low-necked dresses may enhance the appearance of age by wearing a band of black velvet or a choker of jewels about the neck. The hair may be dressed in a different style and combs or jewelry used as ornaments. In fact, special attention should be given to all kinds of jewelry. Old heirlooms from the family treasure chest will often add greatly to the effect of age.

Clothing

An excellent make-up goes for nought unless the proper clothing is chosen for the character. Young men should not make the mistake of appearing in their ordinary clothing if they are to be seen as a middle-aged character. An older, less perfectly fitting suit should be worn. The same holds true with women. An elegant, trimly fitting suit just out of the shop is not going to give the appearance of middle age when worn by a girl. It is better to choose an outfit that has seen some service when playing such parts, preferably by one of the age being portrayed.

Rough characters, whose clothes are apt to be dirty, should not be seen in bright new things. A preparation called "Fuller's Earth" is available at all drug stores and may be dusted over the clothing to give the appearance of soil. It is a harmless, sterile preparation and may be used for any purpose.

Such items as costume come properly within the province of the director or costume designer, but the make-up artist, with propriety, may keep a watchful eye over them to add his bit.

Scrapbooks

The diligent make-up artist will maintain a scrapbook of character types gleaned from the magazines and newspapers. Make-up is always more successful if modelled after a genuine type. The illustrations may be clipped and pasted into the scrapbook under some such classification as exists in this volume. They are then available for ready reference and may be used as models by the make-up artist as he works.

Make-Up Rehearsals

Every make-up used in a play should be seen "out front" by the director or other competent persons before the night of the performance. To this end, it is wise to conduct a make-up rehearsal on the stage on the night preceding the dress rehearsal under the actual lighting conditions that will be used at the time of the performance. There is such variation prevailing in the lights on the average stage that there is no other way of making sure the make-up gives the effect intended. With an early make-up rehearsal, there is ample time to make necessary changes before the performance.

Chapter XV

INDIVIDUAL CHARACTER MAKE-UPS (Male)

By this time, the beginner should have sufficient experience in the art of make-up to proceed through the following repertoire without much difficulty. They are all fashioned, to a great extent, on the different types of make-up outlined previously.

Rough Characters

Tramps: The basic make-up employed here is the one for robust middle age. If the tramp character is to appear somewhat dissipated, this may be done by heightening the shadows under the eyes and by highlighting the little pouch that appears directly under the eye to make it more prominent.

The rough appearance is supplied by the scraggly beard. Crepe hair may be used as outlined in the previous chap-

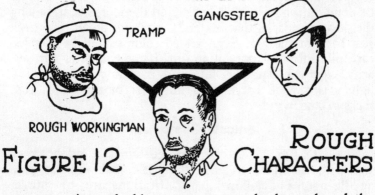

TRAMP

GANGSTER

ROUGH WORKINGMAN

FIGURE 12   ROUGH CHARACTERS

ter, or a piece of old newspaper may be burned and the resulting ash smeared liberally over those portions of the face where the beard would normally be.

With a comedy tramp character, sometimes seen in

vaudeville, these features are merely heightened to the point of burlesque. The pouch under the eye is painted dead white and this and the beard outlined with black. The hair or ash used for the beard may be liberally mixed with dark blue lining color to increase the effect. The nose is also done in bright red.

Thieves and Gangsters: These will vary somewhat depending on the character. The pale make-ups are generally used. For best effect, rouge on the lips and cheeks is eliminated entirely and a little Olive or sallow tinted grease paint blended into the foundation color.

With certain characters, the nose may be twisted slightly out of shape through the use of nose putty, or the effect of a twitching lip may be added by drawing lines about the mouth with a soft lead pencil after the make-up has been completed. (See also Scars in Chapter IV.)

Rough Workingmen: These do not vary greatly from the basic robust make-ups. The juvenile or middle-aged basic make-ups will be used depending, of course, on the age of the character.

Additional grease paint (Dark Sunburn) may be added to give the effect of an outdoor character. This should be done on the nose, the cheeks and the temples, and along the heavy muscle that extends up and down the neck just back of the ear. Such added color should be blended carefully into the foundation tint. If the character customarily wears a hat, the forehead naturally will be of a lighter tint. The hat shades this part of the head from the sun and wind.

Smooth Characters

Characters in this category are customarily indoor types and will, therefore, require the basic make-up for pale middle age. The following classifications are, of course, somewhat arbitrary and can be varied to suit conditions.

Professional Men: This is the "doctor" type. Weight is added to the character usually by employing one or the other of the moustache types described in the previous chapter. The hair, of course, is either grayed at the temples or grayed completely, depending upon the age of the character.

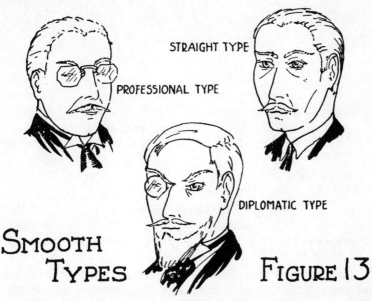

STRAIGHT TYPE

PROFESSIONAL TYPE

DIPLOMATIC TYPE

Smooth Types

Figure 13

Diplomats: The only essential difference between this type and the one above is in the beard. This is applied as indicated in the preceding chapter and smoothly trimmed. The hair is treated as described above.

Eccentric Characters

New England Type: This is the "Uncle Josh" type, once very popular but now seldom seen except in farce comedy. The general characteristics of the type, however, are useful in formulating similar characters.

The old-aged make-up described in Chapter III is the basis of the character. To this is added the goatee formed of white crepe hair and the hair is whitened and the spectacles added. Since such a character is usually humorous it may be well to add two or three "crow's feet" to each outward corner of the eye to impart a merry twinkle.

The Mutton Chop Type: In facial characteristics, this type is similar to the above. The same basic make-up is used. The mouth may be either up or down depending on the character. In place of the goatee, mutton chop whiskers are supplied as outlined in the previous chapter in the section devoted to sideburns.

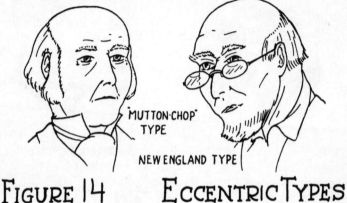

MUTTON-CHOP TYPE

NEW ENGLAND TYPE

FIGURE 14   ECCENTRIC TYPES

Bald-headed wigs may or may not be used with either of these characters. If they are, the frontal piece of the wig is fastened to the forehead as described in the previous chapter. Then, the entire top and frontal piece of the wig is covered with foundation tint of the same shade as that used on the face.

Naturally, the make-up artist will vary all of the characters described in this chapter to suit particular circumstances. It would be impossible to describe a particular make-up for every character seen upon the stage. The artist must use his own judgment and vary the general practice to suit his own particular conception of the character.

Chapter XVI

INDIVIDUAL CHARACTER
MAKE-UPS (Female)

As a general rule, the changes in a woman's make-up are less striking and more subtle than are those of a man. In a modern costume play, the changes of character may be indicated quite as easily by costume as they can by make-up. A few general rules should be kept in mind.

The Society Type

The basis for this make-up may be either the middle-aged or the old-aged make-up described in Chapter III. A more patrician cast to the features may be given by elevating the eyebrows somewhat, blocking out the orig-

FIGURE 15 ⟩ FEMALE TYPES

inal eyebrow and drawing a new one slightly higher on the forehead. The nose may be given a more aquiline and distinguished appearance by highlighting it down the center with a line of white lining color. The line should, of course, be blended carefully into the foundation tint. The hair is grayed as desired and the final touch added by employing either distinguished looking glasses or a lorgnette.

Rough Types

This is a rather arbitrary classification, but frequently, in folk plays or farces such types will be required.

The Washerwoman Type: A variant of the middle-aged basic make-up. The color may be heightened on the cheeks and the face broadened by placing the color outward towards the ears. On occasion, a Light Sunburn powder may be used over the make-up to impart a ruddier cast to the features.

The Rural Type: Many rural types will require no make-ups other than those described for middle-aged or old-aged characters. In instances, though, where the character spends much time out of doors, it will be necessary to deepen the foundation tint. This can be done by applying Olive grease paint to the regular foundation and blending it in to the desired shade. Warts or other irregularities may be added to the features through the use of nose putty.

Eccentric Types

The hag or witch type is encountered most often in fairy plays. It is distinguished by its hook-like nose. If possible, the use of nose putty is to be avoided. The nose and chin may be made more prominent by highlighting them with white lining color. If it cannot be done successfully, the nose putty is molded into shape and applied before the grease paint. An old-aged make-up with very decided highlights and shadows is then used. Frequently, in place of the putty, the nose may be made crooked by following the method outlined in Chapter I for the make-up of the nose.

The Old Maid Type: This is simply an old-aged or middle-aged make-up with special emphasis placed on the lines and shadows about the mouth. They should give the appearance of severity. Of course, it should be remembered that all old maids are not severe. When they are not, the regular make-up will apply. Generally, a somewhat outmoded style of dressing the hair will serve to indicate an old maid type.

Chapter XVII

FANTASTIC MAKE-UPS

Fantastic make-ups are rarely met with in the ordinary course of amateur play production, but the make-up artist will do well to acquaint himself with the procedure to be followed in creating them. Fairy plays employ them frequently, and the knowledge thus gained will aid the artist in creating other types.

Mephistopheles: With this make-up, every effort is made to give a V-shaped quality to the face. The eyebrows and the eyes point upward at their outer edges; so does the mouth and chin.

To begin, the nose and jaw are shaped with nose putty until they attain a sharp and aquiline appearance. The eyebrows may also be blotted out with the same material.

Two types of foundation tint are permissible with this character: One a very pale shade in which no color on the cheeks is used though the lips are bright. In the other, a bright and ruddy complexion is used for the foundation tint. The artist may choose. For the light make-up use a grease paint No. 1 or 2 while for the brighter one, Dark Sunburn is liberally mixed with any flesh tint.

When applying cheek rouge, if used, care should be taken to see that it follows the general V-shaped contour of the face. A rather heavy shading of blue or lavender is applied along the line of the beard to increase the sharpness of the face. The lip rouge is tilted upward at the ends of the mouth as shown (Fig. 16) and the same method followed when lining the eyes and the brows.

A neutral powder (Stein's No. 8) is used for the light make-up while a shade comparable to Light Sunburn may prove useful for the brighter one.

Clowns: Clown white, a special preparation, is generally

used for all clown make-ups though white grease paint will serve just as well and is considerably easier for the inexperienced person to apply.

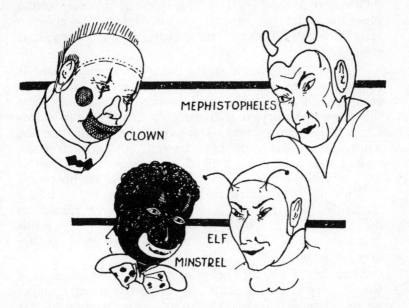

FIGURE 16   FANTASTIC MAKE-UPS

With grease paint, the foundation tint is laid in of dead white and the requisite markings of red, black, or yellow applied directly on top without further ado. With the clown white, it is necessary to draw around the colored parts by placing a small quantity of the material on the tip of the little finger and drawing around these areas. The remainder of the face, the neck, and the ears is then covered with the clown white and the colored markings added afterwards. In both cases, it is necessary to powder the face thoroughly after the make-up is completed to avoid unpleasant messiness.

Clown make-ups are extremely individual; no two are

alike, but however fantastic, the make-up artist will try to give an understandable character, either happy or sad, to each face.

Minstrel Make-Up: The true minstrel make-up comes properly under the heading of the fantastic because no effort is made to give a true picture of the Negro; it is a burlesque.

Prepared burnt cork is the best for amateur use. It is applied with water. The face is dampened, the burnt cork applied and rubbed smooth wherever wanted. After the make-up is dry, it is thoroughly brushed with a cosmetic brush. No powder is applied. The mouth and the white spaces around the eyes are best outlined before the rest of the make-up is applied by taking a small dab of the cork on the tip of the little finger. Use no lip rouge.

With all burnt cork make-ups, it is wise to follow implicitly the directions of the manufacturer placed on the package. To violate these suggestions, may result in a two weeks' job of removing the make-up. It should give no trouble.

Elves and Fairies: The pale, delicate complexion of a female fairy is best indicated by using the straight make-up recommended for blondes in an earlier portion of this book. Every effort should be made to keep the features and coloring as fine and delicate as possible.

Elves and brownies are another matter. These little creatures of the woods usually have the sharp, thin features associated with the character of Mephistopheles described in the beginning of this chapter. The nose and chin are built up through the use of nose putty and an Olive grease paint used for the foundation tint. The eyes and brows are turned upward at the outer edges as was the case with Mephistopheles.

As a matter of fact, there is no limit to the facial tints that may be given these creatures. A tree elf may have a greenish cast to his face while a water sprite may have a blue. These various colorings may be obtained by softening a bit of lining color with cold cream in the palm of the hand and carefully blending it in with the foundation tint.

Antennae, the little "feelers" projecting from the forehead, are made by squeezing a bit of black tooth wax on the end of a short piece of black enameled copper wire. A small loop is bent on the opposite end to assist in fastening it to the forehead and the whole put in place through the use of nose putty.

The Toby: This old-time comedy character has almost disappeared from the boards, but he pops up frequently enough in one form or another to warrant his inclusion here. He is the comedy yokel, the bumpkin of the country crossroads.

Many Toby comedians use no grease paint at all. They simply add a bulbous nose (nose putty), black out a few teeth, add freckles and they are ready for their public. However, if grease paint is used, it should be kept very flat without any lights or shadows. A little white liner may be added around the eyes to increase the expression of stupidity. A frowzy wig completes the make-up.

Such make-ups today have their uses in portraying the comedy hillbilly type.

Chapter XVIII

NATIONALITY MAKE-UPS

There is much useless abracadabra used about the difficulty of making up for the various nationality types. Simplification will serve as well in this type of make-up as with any other. Human beings, of whatever nationality, are much the same and will appear more natural on the stage if an over-elaborate style of make-up is avoided.

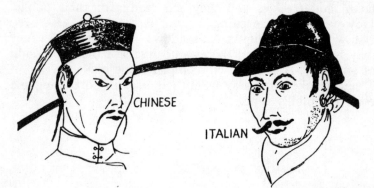

FIGURE 17   NATIONALITY MAKE-UPS

Where the skin is colored, either yellow or brown, the make-up artist will frequently find it easier to supply these colors with liquid make-up rather than grease paint. Such make-up comes in cans or bottles and is easily applied with a small sponge to a smooth, even texture. In any event, the liquid make-up is used on the hands. When dry it will not rub off as the grease paint does except with washing.

Chinese: Light Cinema Tan may be used for the foundation grease paint on Chinese characters although there is no objection to using the various grease paints labeled, Chinese, Mikado, etc. Collies will appear much darker than will Mandarins. An Olive grease paint will serve as foundation for the former.

No cheek or lip rouge is used on male characters though rather full, thick lips may be provided for the females.

If the actor's eyebrows are rather heavy, these should be blocked out as described previously (Chapter IV.) before supplying the slanting brows with liner or an eyebrow pencil. In lining the eyes, every effort should be made to keep them as natural looking as possible. The lining should be dipped downward on the inner edges and upward at the outer corners (See Fig. 17). A small white dot placed on the lower inside corner of the eye will sometimes add to the Oriental effect.

Wigs are usually worn with a Chinese character. If the eyes do not slant sufficiently the corners may be pulled up with adhesive tape placed under the frontal piece of the wig though this is not usually necessary.

Any neutral shade of powder may be used on a Chinese make-up. The same holds true with most other nationality types. Despite the warnings of the make-up companies, it is unnecessary to purchase a comparable powder for every shade of grease paint used.

Before leaving the Chinese character entirely, it may be well to describe the make-up of the sing-song girl or Chinese professional entertainer. For this character, the face is painted a dead white, either with clown white or grease paint, and a large circle of red supplied for each cheek. The eyes are treated as before and the make-up thoroughly powdered.

Italian: The swarthy feature of Italian make-ups is supplied by blending Olive grease paint into the foundation tint and proceeding as usual. The nose may, on occasion, be made more aquiline by highlighting down the center. Moustaches may be provided for the men, while with the peddler type, a roughening of the beard with lining color will prove sufficient. The costumes of Italian characters on the stage are usually so distinctive that any swarthy make-up will immediately be accepted as Italian without further fuss.

Hawaiian: Liquid make-up is recommended for Hawaiian characters. The shade called Gypsy will give the best results. Hawaiian hair is always black. Either a wig should be supplied or the hair treated with mascara. The hair of the men may be curled if so desired to give a somewhat bushy effect.

American Indian: Olive grease paint with a blending of Dark Sunburn will serve as a foundation tint for the Indian though the regular Indian grease paint may be used. The nose is highlighted to make it more prominent and the brows and eyes outlined with black.

War paint is not used indiscriminately on all Indian characters, only when they are on the warpath or engaged in an Indian ceremony. These are supplied with lining colors, red, blue, and yellow.

As before, the liquid make-up of the proper shade is recommended for Indians. Usually so much of the body is displayed that grease paint make-ups serve only to unnecessarily complicate the task. The liquid make-up is used on both body and face. Any other features can be supplied, shading, etc., by using grease paint over the liquid make-up.

Hindu and Moorish: With these make-ups, a foundation grease paint of either Hindu or Othello (Moor) is applied to the face and powdered. No lining of any kind is usually done. The same holds true with the liquid make-up. The general tone of these make-ups is so dark that the effect of any lining is lost.

Japanese: The basis of the Japanese make-up is a foundation tint of either Light Cinema Tan, Olive, or Japanese grease paint. No rouge is used on the lips or cheeks. The eyes of the Japanese do not definitely slant upwards as do the Chinese but a more Oriental effect may be obtained if it is done so slightly. All female characters should wear a wig. The men may wear a wig with the stiff, upstanding pompadour of the Japanese or may blacken their own hair with mascara. The faces of Japanese geisha girls are very white and rouge is applied to the lips and cheeks in a very bright red.

Negro: The minstrel make-up should not be confused with that of the true Negro. Grease paint make-up for this character on the professional stage has almost been

AMERICAN INDIAN

MEXICAN

JAPANESE

FIGURE 18   NATIONALITY MAKE-UPS

entirely discarded in favor of the liquid type. The latter is available in several shades. The correct one should be chosen to fit the character.

As with other dark make-ups, care should be taken to see that the palms of the hands remain much lighter than the backs. The best effect is obtained by wiping the make-up off the palms with a slightly damp sponge after it has been applied to leave a trifle darker shade in the creases of the hand.

Mexican: With Mexicans of the upper classes, it is only necessary to add a faint tint of Olive to the foundation grease paint and proceed as outlined for the straight or character make-ups. Peons or Mexican Indians will require a darker shade, either Olive or Gypsy, for the foundation tint. Sideburns and moustaches or beards may be supplied for the men as needed.

With all nationality make-ups, the facial tints of the women are usually lighter than those of the men. A light pink may be lightly blended into the foundation grease paint or a trifle lighter shade of liquid make-up may be used or the latter need not be applied so heavily. A sufficient distinction can sometimes be made by powdering the women thoroughly with a lighter shade of powder than the men.

In any case, it is not necessary to purchase an elaborate kit of materials to obtain effective make-ups of the principal nationality types. One or two extra grease paint sticks, Olive or Moor, or one or two cans of the liquid make-up in a suitable color are all that is required.

Chapter XIX

BODY MAKE-UP

Make-up is frequently applied to the hands to alter their shape. Grease paint may be used but the newer liquid types of make-up are coming into favor for this purpose because they do not rub off on the clothing.

Make-up of the Hands

SHADOWS

HIGHLIGHTS

Figure 19

The hands may be made to appear more bony by adding shadows between the knuckles as shown in Fig. 19. The effect may be increased by highlighting with a thin, white line along the back of each finger and blending it into the foundation. Warts, swollen knuckles, or other irregularities may be indicated through the use of nose putty. Such a make-up of the hands is used, in varying degrees, to indicate age and on witches or similar characters.

One of the most effective ways to make a youthful body appear older is through the wearing of clothes that have seen some service on an older person. Clothes tend to fit themselves to the shape of the wearer. To a degree, they will retain this shape when worn on another person. An older man's suit will especially help in giving the appearance of age to a younger one.

The figure may be padded in various ways to give more weight. Specially built padding may be rented from costume companies to give the effect of a paunch, but with a little ingenuity, safety pins, and a half dozen Turkish towels, anyone can fashion an acceptable paunch for a character. The paunch should not appear as a decided bump but should·be carefully blended into the figure by pinning the towels in place with safety pins. The ends of the towels should extend a portion of the way around the back.

It is difficult to thicken the legs, but especially built padding may be rented from costume companies. These outfits are called "cylindricals" and are worn like a pair of tights.

In Shakespearean plays, or plays where tights are worn, the wise actor will improve the appearance of his leg by wearing a heavy, worsted pair of tights beneath the outer ones. The same should be done if knee breeches and "opera" or knee length hose are worn. Modern legs may appear ridiculous in such costume. The bony joints may be smoothed away by "underdressing" with these heavy, flesh-colored tights. There is usually no extra charge for the rental of such.

Humped backs may be fashioned by stuffing a towel into the desired position and tying it firmly in place with a long cloth extended around the shoulders and chest.

Careful actresses make up their arms and backs when wearing low cut decollete. Chorus girls do the same with their legs. Liquid make-up is used for this purpose, the lighter shades.

Height may be added to a character by wearing thick heel pads inside the shoe. These are the ordinary pads obtainable in most shoe stores. If insufficient height is gained, it may be necessary to have a shoemaker add a half inch or so to the heels of the shoes.

A one-armed character is achieved by binding the missing arm to the side and across the stomach with wide cloth binds. The same method is employed in eliminating a leg, but for this purpose, it is wiser by far to obtain one of the specially built false legs from a costume company. With the latter, it is imperative to see that the leg is removed from its straps during each intermission of the play to restore circulation.

Chapter XX

LIGHT MAKE-UPS

Light make-ups have their uses on the concert stage and in vaudeville. Here there is usually no need to portray a character. The make-up is used solely to counteract the effect of the lights.

The Concert Make-Up: Make-ups of this type are commonly called dry make-ups. No cold cream base or foundation tint is used. A little cold cream is placed on the upper lid of each eye and the eye made up as detailed for the straight make-up. Dry rouge of the appropriate shade is placed on the cheeks by using a powder puff or rabbit's foot. Women may use rouge on the lips; men seldom do. The make-up is then powdered, sometimes by mixing a little Light Sunburn powder into the customary neutral shade if the make-up appears too pale. If necessary, the dry rouge on the cheeks is touched up again after the powder has been used.

Besides the concert stage, make-ups like the above have their uses when large groups of people, choruses, etc., are to be made up and insufficient time is available for a grease paint job. The make-up should be carefully blended as with other types.

The Vaudeville Make-Up: Vaudeville performers frequently work very close to the footlights. A variant of the ordinary straight make-up has been developed for these cases. It is mostly worn by men. Women employ the concert make-up described above.

The make-up is similar to the straight variety except that no rouge is used on the cheeks or lips. A somewhat ruddier cast is imparted to the whole by lightly blending in either Olive or Sunburn grease paint into the foundation tint. Much of the same effect, however, may be obtained on a lighter foundation by powder with a darker powder, Sunburn or Olive.

With the above make-up, the grease paint is applied as thinly as possible. It is employed by acrobats, comedians, and vaudeville singers.

Arena Stage Make-Ups: Make-ups for the arena stage depend to a large extent on the quantity of light available. If the area is flooded with a large amount of light, considerable make-up can be used. If not, the make-ups will have to be less heavy since, under normal conditions, the audience will be seated quite close to the actors.

For straight make-ups, use as little grease paint as possible. Stick to dry rouge, powder and a heightening of the eyebrows and the eyes with a make-up pencil, if necessary.

However, with character make-ups, the problem is somewhat different. Grease paint must be used. Even so, it is not advisable to use a lot of it or to produce plays in which heavy character make-ups are essential unless a substantial quantity of light is available. If there is light, in good quantities, it is surprising how much make-up can be applied.

Amber in a few of the floods, for instance, has a strong tendency to wash out many of the colors which are applied on the face. By using a little amber in the lighting system for the arena area, it is possible to strike a happy medium and use a considerable amount of character make-up and not have it become objectionable or too obvious to the audience.

It is advisable to avoid the use of lines as much as possible. Work from the various planes of the face as suggested earlier. To indicate age, change the contours of the face and blend the colors very carefully, using relatively less of them than would be done under normal stage conditions. Powder the hair very carefully or use white mascara for grayness. Use the system recommended in this book but use it with more subtlety.

It is essential that the make-up be tried out at an advance rehearsal if there is the least bit of doubt as to how it will appear under performance conditions. Since arena staging is often done in halls where the lighting system is only remotely adapted to stage presentation, such precautions are necessary.